# Praise for *Free at Last*:

"At times, it is raw. At times, it is remarkable. At every turn, Marcel's story will rivet your heart to the possibilities in life regardless of where you have come from. Marcel's journey will challenge you to grasp the power of the vows you make, the priority of personal growth, and the need for purpose that outlasts all the obstacles and accomplishments of life. This is a must-read for anyone who wants to believe they can become more than they are today!"

- Bill Farrell, Best-selling Author of *Men Are Like Waffles, Women Are Like Spaghetti*

*"Free At Last* is a gripping, brutally honest, and extremely raw page turner. Certainly, not your typical rags-to-riches story by any stretch of the imagination.

"Becker courageously takes his readers on an emotional, dark, and brutally honest journey through his own personal hell. A journey filled with climatic downfalls as well as triumphs. From poverty and abuse, gangs, drugs, and prison, to repeatedly escaping death, to fatherhood, to realizing his own self-worth, to finally using his talents for the purpose they were generously gifted to him for.

Masterfully written. A MUST read."

- Dee Lortt Dean, *East County Herald*

"The impact of Marcel Becker's book *Free at Last* can only be outdone by watching him live. His generosity, wisdom, and love in the community has transformed El Cajon in the same way he was radically transformed. I am blessed to know him, and the world will be blessed by his story being told for generations."

- Phil Ortiz, El Cajon City Councilmember

"I've just read through *Free at Last* for the second time and it was just as gripping as it was the first time, impossible to put down. It's a story of redemption, love, loss, heartache and triumph that probably only a handful of people in this world could truly relate to but something everyone can appreciate. I challenge anybody finishing this book not to come away feeling good about the faith and power in overcoming all things through Christ. A remarkable and powerful testimony that should really help others."

- Mike Harrison, Former Chief of Staff for Congressman Hunter

"In the four years I have known Marcel professionally, he has been a focused businessman with an intense interest and concern for every employee, customer, and associate. Reading *Free at Last*, I struggled to align the character in the book and the man I know today. His message should be a guiding light to persons lost and without direction in their lives – God can change people and their environment. I was riveted to the story and am proud to count Marcel as a friend."

- Gene Blevins, American Bureau of Shipbuilding

"A true testament to what the human soul can endure! A guide for anyone who has ever been on the wrong side of the tracks and is seeking the path back to righteousness – and a beacon of hope for those who have not yet started the journey back. Where most reside in the decisions they have made, Marcel wanted more. He became a titan of industry, an honorable man, father, grandparent, and an inspiration for us all. If you know anyone who needs a new perspective on life, they have to read this book!"

- Kirk Boettner, Cal Marine

"*Free At Last* is a powerful account of one man's fight with demons, soul searching, strength, and redemption. His writing style is straightforward while finding humor in the ironies of life. Marcel is a man of contradictions who makes it all work due to his underlying strength."
- Joe Pritchard, Retired GM, NASSCO

"Marcel Becker's life is a story that reads like a novel. It is rare that a person faces the challenges that Marcel has and comes out the other side alive. Marcel is that rare person. Because he is willing to share the journey, those that may be close to giving up can find strength to believe in an ever-since-then day of redemption.

This book is a hazardous roadmap that ends up in a crescendo of divine purpose. It powerfully spells out what can happen when God and man decide they would not give up on each other. If you are in need of hope that is just outside your reach, consume this book; it is an introduction to overcoming faith."
- Kevin Miller, Administrative Pastor, Foothills Christian Church

In an age of safe spaces and political correctness, Marcel's raw and honest story is refreshing. At times it makes you want to wince; by the time you're finished it fills you with hope.
- Reed Uberman, IndieThinker

Once I started reading *Free at Last* I could not stop. While written in plain language, Marcel Becker's journey spoke to my heart. *Free at Last* is not a book I would normally pick up but I am so grateful I did.
- Senator Joel Anderson, Ret.

# Excerpts of Letters from Ex-Cons:

"Mr. Becker, just hearing your story gives me hope."
- D.H.

"Mr. Becker, I'd like to thank you for your presentation today. It is very interesting to hear about someone that was once in my situation – and to know about your success is very inspiring. Thank you."
- V.A.

"Dear Mr. Becker, I really want to thank you for all your time and the experiences you shared with us. It was really a motivation for me and an eye-opener. I was happy I was able to relate to you in a sort of way that made me have some kind of hope for my future and to know that there is a second chance for me."
- K.D.

"Mr. Marcel Becker, your story today left me very inspired. Your serious past history in the justice system assured me that I am not alone, and I was very surprised that your past did not stop you from getting to where you are now. [Your story] has made me a better man today. Thank you so much."
- J.A.P.

"Dear Marcel Becker, thank you so much for coming in and showing everyone that your past doesn't determine your future. You're a perfect example of what I'm striving to be."
- S.Z.

Cover Art by
Emilie Hendryx, EAHCreative.com

Author Photo by
Cindie Wolfe, Own the Moments Photography

First published in the United States of America


ISBN: 978-0-578-89887-2

Published by Mephibosheth and Co.
Tunnel Hill, GA 30755

For news and updates from Marcel, visit
https://mailchi.mp/75f2f0b9a093/free

## Other Books by W.A. Fulkerson:

*For Whom the Sun Sings*

*Writing With Purpose: A Step-By-Step Guide to Producing Your Best Book*

# Free at Last

*by*

Marcel Becker

with W.A. Fulkerson

# Chapter 1

Well, I guess you could say my trouble started early.

Most kids growing up in the U.S. during the 1960s were proud to have a father who served in World War II, but for me it was a closely guarded secret. You see, my dad fought for the Germans. You think bullying is bad if you wear glasses? Imagine what would have happened to me if anyone found out that Dad had been in the Wehrmacht.

To his credit, he was not what you'd call an enthusiastic supporter. Dad was nineteen years old when he was conscripted into the German army and shipped off to Russia. He was old enough to remember when Germany was different, when five-year-olds didn't spend every free moment getting brainwashed in Hitler Youth programs. This created something of a social rift, in fact, because my dad's close friend "Hans" had a diverging perspective, being a few years younger and having grown up in the brainwashing program. He drank the Kool-Aid, you might say, which explains how Hans ended up in the SS as a rearguard against deserters and my dad got sent to Russia to freeze to death. To make matters worse, Dad got caught.

The Russians took him captive while he was on patrol one night, and brought him back to their lines as a prisoner. And if being in a Russian military prison during wartime sounds unpleasant to you, believe it or not it was better than being with the Nazi army on that frozen, godforsaken stretch of wilderness. The Russians wanted information, naturally, but lucky for my dad, he was able to escape, and he returned to the loving arms of the Fatherland's army.

The welcome was not all that warm. The officers weren't buying the whole "kidnapped by the Russians" story, and he was accused of being a deserter. He denied it, they insisted, and then they marched him in front of a firing squad, put his back against the wall, and aimed the guns.

*Click.*

He was still alive, somehow. He must've checked himself for bullet holes, and finding none, had to have been thoroughly confused, as well as a nervous wreck. They had dry-fired on him in an attempt to break his resistance, in order to get him to admit that he had deserted and was now working as a spy.

The only problem was, none of that was true. They had no evidence to the contrary, but being Nazis, they weren't exactly the generous type. He was reinstated into the army, but he was put right back at the front, in the midst of the heaviest fighting at the tip of the spear. Now, we aren't certain if Dad was purposely placed in a "punishment squad" (which is German for "cannon fodder") or not, but the fact is that he was placed where the carnage was the worst and fresh soldiers were constantly needed to make up for the casualties.

People didn't generally live long in these sorts of assignments.

Long story short, he survived somehow. As the war was seeming to come to a close in Europe, my dad was terrified of being captured by the Soviets. He understood that coming into their hands again was no better than a death sentence, and he was likely to never be seen or heard of again. So, he made his way to Innsbruck, Austria, which was neutral territory at the time, and he waited for the Americans to arrive. Sure enough, Uncle Sam came through, and my dad was happy to surrender. He liked America, and he was relieved that the war, for him, would be over. American P.O.W. camps naturally beat Russian prisons and German punishment squads, but it makes me take a step back to stop and think what life must have been like for my old man that being a prisoner of war was a rest from his troubles.

The war ended, and Dad went back to Cologne, where he was from. It was rubble. Being one of the westernmost German cities, it had been a regular target of British and other Allied bombing raids. It was completely destroyed, with 95 percent of the population having fled. Before the war, it had a population of around a million people. After, there were only fifty thousand. The place he had known ever since childhood was gone – a post-apocalyptic parody of itself.

His wife had married another man. The life expectancy of a German soldier on the Russian front was only about two years, and since he had been gone quite a bit longer than that, she had assumed he was dead. I suppose you can't blame her for that. We aren't quite sure what happened when he showed up at her doorstep, but we do know that when he left, he understood that his wife and his son were no longer his own.

So, after being shot at, captured, abused, scarred, abandoned, rejected, beaten, chewed up, and spit out, my dear old dad decided that the European continent had nothing left for him, and he ended up in Chicago to start a new life.

Evidently you can't just walk away from that kind of trauma, however. My dad suffered severely from Post-Traumatic Stress Disorder (PTSD) before anyone ever called it that, or really regarded it much at all. He was an intense, violent, and angry man. To be perfectly honest, I didn't like him all that much – and that's putting it mildly. He was a bad father to me, as I'll get into in more detail later. Nevertheless, I believe every man deserves a fair treatment, and I don't think it would be fair to tell you what he was like to me without first explaining a little bit about why he was the way that he was.

It is everyone's responsibility in life to rise above their circumstances, and in at least several key areas, my father did not do that. But though it is hard for me to feel compassion for him, I can at least have understanding. I can only hope that the people I've hurt over the years might have that same understanding for me.

## The Chef de Cuisine

My mother, on the other hand, was a saint. She'd had her share of adversity, but she handled it a different way. She married the devil, so maybe that was her vice, but you'd never meet a kinder, gentler woman in your life. She was born in Switzerland, the oldest of eight children, and a belligerent in a nasty bout with childhood polio that left her significantly disabled and slightly disfigured. One of her legs was a good bit shorter than the other, and she had very little use in one of her hands. She wanted to be a foreign language interpreter, but her father told her that he needed to provide for the seven other kids coming up, so he couldn't afford to send her to college. Instead, she was fated to become a cook, and like everything else she ever set her hand to, she excelled at it.

She became a chef de cuisine, trained in the fine art of French cooking, and believe me when I tell you she was a magician in the kitchen. They say if you perform brilliantly in your craft that you'll perform for kings, and that was true for my mother. She ended up coming to America and working as the private chef for an Italian count in Texas. His name was Count Rodolfo Crespi, a major figure in the fashion industry, and because my mother was fluent in Italian and a highly trained chef, she got the job. The famous opera singer Marie Callas was a frequent guest of the Crespi estate, and my mother had occasion to meet and serve her as well.

She met my father, and for some reason they fell in love. Mom overcame polio, learned six languages, was literally a world-class chef despite some very real physical limitations, and she always had a cheerful, get-to-work attitude and a loving compassion for others. Then there was my father: frequently out of work, paranoid, intense, and violent. I never understood how someone like mom could love someone like dad. Living with the two of them was like having a pillow made of cotton and a mattress made of nails. I preferred the pillow.

I suppose my mother did solve the mystery of how she came to love such a man, however. According to my brother, she used to say that my dad was the only person in the world who could make her feel whole and not handicapped. He made her feel like she wasn't disfigured, and I guess that is a little silver lining in the cloud of doom that came to dominate my childhood.

I don't think I'll ever fully understand their relationship, but this unlikely pairing is what gave life to my older brother, Mike, and four years later, to me.

# Chapter 2

Shortly after giving birth to me, I suppose mom got homesick, because the family packed up and moved back to Europe. As a consequence, German happens to be my first language, despite having spent the vast majority of my life in America. The main reason we returned to the U.S. after a few years abroad is that my father did not want to be in Europe. The devastation from the war was still all-too-evident, as were the bad memories. He was a U.S. citizen by this point, and he loved America. The future seemed more promising across the pond, and it seemed to my folks that children who were born in the U.S. ought to grow up there, too.

And there's the fact that Europe's cold weather was bad for my mother's disability. Her legs didn't work too well, not in the normal way that people walk, at least, and any time there was ice on the ground, she was virtually a prisoner of the house. By necessity, she couldn't go outside for three or five months out of the year. So, when my parents decided to move back to the states, they chose a different sort of climate. That's how we ended up in sunny Oceanside, California.

We lived in a little duplex on a half lot at Tait Street, complete with blue trim and a driveway. There was a little grass and a lot of dirt, some plants here and there. When I was old enough, I even planted a palm tree in a five-gallon bucket and put it in the yard. It was pretty close to the beach, which was a plus. Mike and I shared a bedroom, and Mom and Dad had the other room in our two bed, one bath abode.

If this all sounds glamorous to you, allow me to educate you on a little bit of history. Oceanside in the 1960s and

70s was not the bourgeois paradise that it is today, dotted with multimillion-dollar homes and whatnot. Parts of it were nice enough, but "the bad part of town" was half the town. Back in my day, large swaths of Oceanside were made up of what the government called "affordable housing" and I call "the projects." The whole community sprang up in the first place because of the military base at Camp Pendleton, so instead of plazas and shopping malls, there was a railroad yard and a sewage treatment plant. We moved in 1966, so the Vietnam War was going on, and besides all the unrest that went along with that, in 1975 the Fall of Saigon happened, which meant a huge influx of refugees and tent cities. Put it all together and you have a crowded, small community of largely-impoverished, desperate individuals.

Upstanding members of society generally opted to live somewhere else.

Today, Oceanside is all gentrified. They're building houses that are worth more than the whole block I grew up on, and that's no exaggeration. But back then, I guess people hadn't yet figured out it was prime real estate. Funny how a place can be rundown because people don't see any value in it. Once they see value, it changes drastically.

So, let me tell you what a typical day was like when I was a kid:

I was rumbled awake by the early morning train heading south, and then, throughout the course of the day, the helicopters flew over my house from dawn till dusk. It was like the opening scene of *Apocalypse Now,* all day. And then, when the breeze quit blowing in the evening, we'd get the smells from the uncovered sewage plant, and then the trains would rumble me to sleep at night.

So, it was trains waking you up, helicopters keeping you up, and when the helicopters finally stopped, there was the undeniable scent of defecation to make you wish that the trains would stop running long enough for you to fall asleep and drift off to the land where the streets are paved with gold and no one has a nose. This was where I grew up.

On one side of our tiny home, the neighbors were Black Panthers, and on the other side, bikers from a gang called the Mescaleros. In fact, one of my earliest memories was of sitting in the driveway, playing with a toy truck in the dirt, playing bulldozer and making little roads, when I heard some yelling. It was one of the bikers, a redhead named Evil with a big, ZZ Top kind of beard. He'd gotten into a fight with his old lady, and it must have hit a boiling point because all of a sudden she was out in the street running and he was chasing her. We didn't have a fence or anything, so this chick ran right past me with a look of total fear on her face, and once she was gone, here comes Evil with a look of total rage. She must have thrown her keys at him or something, because he was leaking a steady river of blood from a cut in his forehead. I was paralyzed, watching them, and all I could think was that this guy was the baddest of the bad.

That sort of scene was not unusual in my neighborhood. It was my first impression of a biker, and in retrospect, thinking that everyone was afraid of this guy may have affected my later choices and indiscretions.

It was a rough neighborhood, so I mostly entertained myself. I went fishing as often as I could. The railroad tracks were my playground, and I liked to hunt around for things people might have tossed off of the train. I'd put nails on the tracks and wait for a train to come by and flatten them. There was a mobile storage place near our duplex, and they always left big crates and boxes lying around, so I'd build forts and find other kids to play tag in between these mazes we would make. It wasn't all bad.

The food wasn't great.

We were on welfare a lot growing up, so we subsisted on cauliflower, cabbage, potatoes, and that ersatz invention known as government cheese. Thank God my mom was a chef, because she could make a soup out of these things that made it endurable. Sweet woman that she was, she'd even cook for the bikers down the street because none of them knew how to cook, but they still needed to eat. So, there we were on the dregs of welfare, and mom was still giving.

Since we were near the military base, we also got some MREs, or rations like the soldiers got. There were all different kinds, and they came in these little green cans. If you were one of the cool kids, you had a pocket can opener so that you could dig into one of these whenever you wanted. My favorite ration had saltine crackers and dark chocolate in it. That combination never made sense to me – I guess Uncle Sam was making sure the soldiers mixed their salts and sweets – but we'd collect as many of these cans as we could and trade them with the other kids. Anything to avoid having to eat more government cheese.

We were poor, and there was unrest and violence in the neighborhood from time to time, but a lot of people are poor and still happy. Sure, there was constant noise and smells and filth, but it wouldn't have been all that terrible if not for one other thing that was in Oceanside: my dad.

# Chapter 3

My father, once a soldier, then just a lost soul trying to make his way in a new nation, was a machinist by trade, but that doesn't mean he worked often. He was laid off several times, quit others, and just couldn't seem to get up the energy or the faith to go out and make something happen during the other times. His provision was on-again, off-again, with more off than on. He was skilled as a machinist and wanted to work, but as a consequence of the war and the traumas he had endured early in life, by the time I was ten years old, my dad had suffered two heart attacks, was blind in one eye, and was missing a finger, in addition to being mentally ill. He was fifty-three years old and severely impaired. When times got tough and someone needed to be let go from the payroll, Dad was always at the top of the list, due to his limitations.

The closest thing to regular work that he did was drag my sorry butt out of bed at 2:00 a.m. on Friday and Saturday mornings and make me walk along the pier, in the alleys, and dive into dumpsters to collect aluminum cans so he could turn them in for money at the recycling plant. I hated doing this. Even at a young age, I knew there was something wrong about making a seven-year-old pull half-empty beer cans out of the hands of drunk Marines at 2:00 a.m. We'd go to all the party areas, step over passed-out soldiers, collect for hours, and then I had to crush all of the cans. The family's reward for this slog was a whopping seven cents per pound, but that was a major influx of cash to the Becker household. I imagine this ignoble task was a source of great frustration to my dad, and he knew a lot about frustration.

# Two Brothers, Two Paths

Dad, being the out-of-work, angry man that he was, was no great role model to begin with, but what defined our relationship was something else. Nearly every day he'd find a reason to beat the living daylights out of me. He was a brutal guy, and I was his punching bag. Now, here's the puzzling part: Dad had two sons living with him in that little place on Tait Street – Mike and me – but for some reason he had decided that Mike was alright, and I was a screw up. He chose me to bear his frustrations, to be the bad son. He didn't hit Mike. He hit me.

Even today, decades later as a somewhat enlightened adult, my first thought about the matter is always that the problem somehow originated with me. That I, as a small child, couldn't toe the line right, or I wasn't a good enough student, or some other flaw, but the truth is, none of those explanations make any sense. There's no good reason for it, no explanation that'll satisfy, just the plain truth that Dad decided to love one son and brutalize the other.

I was terrified of him. He was the embodiment of fear. Nothing was ever good enough; I was a disappointment, and everything was open to criticism – and criticism turned physical really quick.

I remember one time when I was a kid that the gasoline rationing was going on. That meant people had to wait in long lines at gas stations to get their allotment for the week, something nobody liked doing.

Well, there I was mowing the lawn, when I ran out of gas. I took a gas can to the pump, and as I was filling up, I had an idea: I could fill up my gas can and then walk out to cars in the back of the line and sell it at a premium to people who hated waiting. Some people were even pushing their cars because they'd run out of gas already, and they were sure to take me up on my offer.

Clearly, I had a head for business. My first enterprise was a monumental success. I came home after the first day with a big grin and a fistful of cash.

Dad assumed I'd stolen the money. He didn't believe it when I told him about my idea and running gasoline back and forth all day in the sun. What should have been a rousing success was a breeding ground for resentment, a chance to tell me I was a criminal, and an excuse for another beating.

Don't misunderstand, I know that I am fully responsible for the crimes I went on to commit later in life. Everyone is liable for their own actions, and that's all there is to it, but the old adage that "wounded people wound people" is really true. Looking back at my old wounds, the dirt that I did in later years starts to make a little more sense, just like my dad's PTSD probably had a hand in his violent temperament.

In any case, I learned early on that I was a screw-up, innovating ideas would end worse than not trying at all, and that my dad was going to hurt me.

Life wasn't all peaches and cream for my brother, either, but for some reason I got the brunt of my dad's wrath. Mike had a very different experience than I did and had some different formative memories. He was embarrassed by the times when we did not have enough money for basic necessities, and he made a vow early on that no matter what he had to do, he would never, ever be poor.

He was as good as his word. Mike went on to do very well in school and achieved considerable success in his chosen profession.

Vows are powerful things; I've come to find out. They shape our mindsets, dictate patterns of behavior, mold our subconscious tastes, desires, and goals. I've made three of them in my life, and each one set a drastic course correction from the way things had been before, with far-reaching consequences.

My formative memory wasn't the lack of money, like Mike remembers; it was of getting smacked around every day. I made a promise early on like my brother did, however, deep in my heart.

I decided that once my father died, I would never, ever be afraid of another living, breathing human being ever again. People were going to fear me.

# Chapter 4

Believe it or not, I was not by nature a troubled student.

In fact, up until high school I was in advanced classes and did pretty well. Today they'd call it advanced placement or say I was an honor's student. Back then it was called being a "mentally gifted minor." Anyway, it all fell apart in high school.

I don't think I lost any ability. I just wasn't willing to put up with the charade anymore. My upbringing had convinced me that I was a failure anyway, every effort ended with the same response from my dad, and I was just tired of playing the game.

And I was getting tired of the beatings. I didn't want to put up with any of it.

At age fourteen, I heard my dad tell me, "One of us is going to have to leave, and it's not going to be me." So, I left. My mother eventually cajoled my father into tracking me down a few days after that to bring me home, but I never really lived with them again. I came and went, but I was gone from that house far more often than I was in it.

I did odd jobs, and when I was fifteen, I got a gig as a dishwasher at a restaurant called "Across the Tracks" (today it's called "McCabe's"). They let me rent out the attic to sleep in, which was furnished with a bed and a couple of chairs, so I had my four walls. My grades in school began to suffer, largely due to my absence. I didn't know what I was going to do, just that I wanted to get away.

## Cobra Kai

I took my vow of never being afraid of anyone ever again quite seriously, and so the first time I got the chance to start learning marital arts, I leaped at the opportunity. If I wanted to be the baddest of the bad, I figured I needed to know something about fighting.

It happened like this. A friend of mine had two brothers and a dad that shared a similarity to my own: He had terrible, undiagnosed PTSD. He'd been special forces in Vietnam, and by the time I was around, it had taken its toll on his psyche. Nevertheless, he was a martial arts expert, and he trained me and his three sons in multiple styles, including Tang Soo Do, Taekwondo, and Okinawan Kenpo Karate. In addition to these traditional arts, in which he was quite accomplished, he also trained us in "pain compliance" maneuvers. I received several years of training this way without having to dish out any money, but I paid heavily for it, if you get my drift.

This Vietnam spook was sadistic with us kids. He was very big on discipline and respect for the dojo (i.e., their garage). The philosophy was "you get it until you've got it," and by "get it" I mean you'd get kicked, punched, swept, or whatever again and again until you learned how to stop it. He was relentless.

At first, it was kind of cool. The brothers that I trained with were already weary with the whole thing because for them it was an obligation. For me, it was scary but intriguing. Eventually, however, I too grew weary of this sort of daily training.

Their dad was keen on us being able to break boards using a variety of strikes. What a lot of people don't know about breaking boards is that it doesn't hurt so much if you succeed. Your force goes through the wood and essentially blows out the other side. If you do not succeed in breaking the board, however, the board literally snaps back, and you are struck back with all of your force. "For every action there is an equal and opposite reaction," right? Hitting a piece of wood without breaking it is very painful, and this guy would never let us stop or try again a different day. We were to strike and strike and strike until we finally got it. Well, on this one day, we were doing an elbow strike to break a board, and I just couldn't wrap my head around the move. I tried over and over because my instructor wouldn't let me stop. I remember crying because my arm was literally purple from my wrist to my elbow and covered in welts. I had to bash my bruised arm meat until I finally broke the stupid board.

This is not the sort of intensity you use with children. The way he trained us would be the intensity you trained soldiers with during wartime, maybe. It was pretty terrifying, but I still learned. Eventually, I could break five boards with my elbow, and more with kicks. I paid a high price to acquire that talent, getting hit over and over again and endlessly performing repetitive motions to master the moves.

It was definitely a "Cobra Kai" sort of situation (from *Karate Kid*), and for now I'll just leave it at that. Wounded people wound people. At least I got some skills out of it.

Of course, it was the martial arts ability that would be my entrance into a formal life of crime. I probably would have ended up there anyway, as I had a lot of angst, confusion, and anger inside of me. My friends and I started experimenting with drugs and alcohol early on, and as a teen I did plenty of boosting (for you strait-laced folks out there, that's a polite way of saying "stealing"). We had the Coors beer distributor right in our back yards at the rail station, and we routinely broke into the rail cars to liberate several cases of beer, which we hid in the crawl spaces underneath neighbors' houses. Ultimately, we'd sell our contraband to a place called Habib's and Achmed's Liquor Store – what we didn't drink, that is.

But the martial arts ability made me stand out. I was fueled by a promise, by inner turmoil and sadistic training, so I gained in skill and prominence quickly. I moved on from working out in the crazy Vietnam vet's backyard to training under the legendary Chuck Hawkins of the American Taekwondo Association. I was head and shoulders above my peers. They were bigger than me, older than me, and more experienced, but my experience wasn't sparring in some cute ring with gloves on and equal footing. I was used to fighting for my life, with no referee, no rules, and no certainty. Coming up as a scared kid, I was now an angry teen, and that anger made me powerful. The first underground fight I had was in some warehouse against an ATA black belt. He never stood a chance. I knocked him out so quickly that the guys began calling me "Flash," a nickname that's stuck with me ever since.

## Escalation

For many people, martial arts are a way of sublimating negative thoughts and feelings, a path to finding peace through a constructive outlet for aggression. For me, it was something different. I loved to fight. I hoped some junkie would mess with me on the street so that I could dominate him. I itched for the underground fights that I would participate in and win.

I was well on my way to becoming the baddest of the bad. Some people did fear me, then. I could see it in their eyes. At this early stage, it was satisfying seeing that look.

Before UFC was on television, complete with referees, sponsors, and people watching with hotdogs via pay-per-view, MMA was underground. We called it cage fighting. Basically, you get two guys, lock them in a cage, and open it up when one of them isn't getting up anymore. Martial arts styles clashed in spectacular fashion. Wrestlers threw kung fu guys. Limalama practitioners kicked judokas. It was dynamic and exciting, and there I was in the middle of it.

I did well – well enough to get noticed by a shady acquaintance of mine who approached me after a fight one night. Let's call this gentleman "Brad."

Brad walked up to me and said, "Hey, Flash, you're pretty good with your hands." It was a statement, but the way he said it, it was like a question.

"Yeah, thanks," I said.

"You know, you could use that to help me out – and make some money for yourself too."

You see, Brad was a drug dealer, a businessman, of sorts, and one of his customers wasn't paying up on a debt. In the underworld, there are financial transactions, loans, sales, distribution, transportation, and the whole network that you see in strait-laced society, but there's a major difference. There are no courts adjudicating disputes, no police to call when someone rips you off, no insurance to back your stash, and when someone doesn't pay what they owe... Well, it still needs to be dealt with. Brad wasn't a killer, but he wouldn't be in business long if word got out that he was an easy mark, that people could leave off of paying him without consequences. So, he reached out to me to go and collect some money for him.

I'll skip the details, but suffice it to say, my martial arts skills made me good at my job. Brad got paid.

"No man chooses evil because it is evil; he only mistakes it for happiness, the good he seeks." That's what Mary Wollstonecraft says, at least. Now, experience tells us that she is wrong in this particular quotation because she puts it in absolute terms that give us an unjustifiably rosy picture of human nature. I have chosen evil because it was evil on many occasions. So have you, and if you think you haven't, then you are blind to your own vices. However, there is a salient point to what Ms. Wollstonecraft says as well. People don't usually head down a dark road with the intention of ruining their life. Usually there is some promise of happiness or betterment. Where crime is concerned, usually that promise is a lie.

When I started doing jobs for Brad, I thought it was a big leg up for me. I thought it would lead to respect, that it would put some money in my pocket and help me get out of dead-end gigs. And just like that, I was in collections. Just like that, I'd crossed the invisible line between adolescent mischief and organized crime. It wouldn't stop there, however. I still had a long, dark road to the bottom.

# Chapter 5

Collections was a booming business. After doing some jobs for Brad, I came to realize that there was a world of opportunity for an enterprising, violent young man such as myself. There were plenty of meth cooks and middleman dealers who didn't know which side of a bat to hold, but they needed their associates to know that they meant business, that there were consequences for holding out on them. Collections seemed like a good way to make some money, and it provided the action I craved.

I was an adult at this point, eighteen or nineteen, and my day job had its own shadiness as well. I was working at an equipment rental company where the boss taught me how to drive trucks and operate machinery. The boss' son taught me how to do lines of cocaine, which we did together regularly.

Funny thing about cocaine is, aside from really twisting up the reward center of your brain, it costs money. Expanding my fledgling roster of clients as a collector seemed like the thing to do.

I realized that commissions weren't the only way to make a buck. Instead of getting a percentage to go out and collect money for some hustler, I could approach these guys and offer to buy their debts. They were usually only too happy to get some kind of return on what seemed like a toxic loan, so I was paying pennies on the dollar for information and the right to collect. I began to get a reputation, and collecting started to pay better than fueling trucks did.

I was still in Oceanside, which benefited my criminal enterprise in an unusual way. Oceanside has a sister city in Samoa called Pago-Pago, and there's actually a sizeable Pacific Islander population there. I ended up studying

Limalama, a Polynesian martial art, because of it, and I briefly went to school with David Seau, the brother of hall-of-fame linebacker Junior Seau. All that to say, I was tight with a lot of Samoans, and my network was inside of theirs. Come to find out, years later, the authorities who were trying to figure out what I was up to just didn't put it together that this white kid was working with a bunch of Pacific Islanders.

That isn't to say that I didn't catch some heat, of course. I was eighteen the first time I got arrested, and it would be far from an isolated incident. I did short stays in jail for possession, but nothing lengthy, and I was always back on the streets again doing my usual dirt. In the circles I ran in, if a sentence was less than a year, we didn't even count it.

One stay in the Vista County Jail, however, was notable.

## Tank Captain

I'd gotten picked up for possession of illegal substances – namely, drugs. I'd been to jail before, and I figured it enhanced my image as a dude you don't want to mess with, so I really wasn't too worried about it. Besides, I'd gotten a bit of a reputation among even the corrections officers.

You see, in jails, they arrange inmates according to cell blocks, or "tanks," and each tank has an inmate liaison, or a guy who is in charge. He's appointed by the corrections officer as "tank captain," and he's expected to keep the other guys in line. Even in prison, inmates squabble over territory and who has what rights to hustle certain things, and these squabbles often get violent. So, alpha dog that I was, the corrections officers soon realized that I wouldn't put up with anyone questioning my authority or toughness, and they thought to put that to their advantage by making me tank captain.

I didn't mind. I liked being in charge, and my philosophy with the guys inside was that the cell block was our domain, and any time the corrections officers were inside our domain, it was a violation of our space. So, the best thing we could do was line up on time, shut up, and not give them any reasons to hang around inside our domain. If they weren't suspicious of us, we could get them off our backs and not have to worry about getting harassed.

There were two kinds of tank captains: gangster and good. By gangster, I mean that certain tank captains would run rackets off of their position: taxing food, charging rent for staying in their cell block, and all of that nonsense. The other kind was guys like me, who didn't use the whole tank captain thing to squeeze anybody. In fact, whenever one of our guys went to court, we guarded their tray and kept it on the rack to make sure they got to eat when they got back. I might not have been a good guy, but I was a good leader in the tank. We took care of our population and gave equal privileges to the different racial groups inside, which was a big deal in jail.

So, despite the fact that I was a prolific offender on the outside, on the inside, I ran a tight ship whenever I was tank captain. They would actually move me around whenever I got a troubled cell block running well, too. Here's how it would go:

I'd get moved to a new tank where the inmates had a power struggle and were causing a lot of problems, and the officers would say I was tank captain. Some of the inmates would disagree with this imposition of authority, but I'd get things settled with two quick hits. The first hit was my fist in somebody's face, and the second was that guy hitting the floor. Then everything was settled, and everybody seemed to pay attention to my reforms. The deputies knew that whenever they put me in a new tank as captain, there'd be a few guys coming out on stretchers, but they just looked the other way. After all, they put me there to do just that, I think, knowing that's what it would take to get the fighting to stop. Then, just when I got things running right, they'd move me to another tank where the inmates were acting up and acting stupid. I wasn't going to put up with that in my tank, so I'd have to start all over again. The deputies got some use out of me, that's for sure.

Well, one time in Vista, we had a problem.

I was on the second floor in a block of cells, as a new tank captain, and I thought I finally had everything squared away, but I knew that a certain racial group in my tank was not happy.

Let me stop for a moment and explain myself. I'm not somebody who discriminates on the basis of race. I think whether you're black, white, orange, or green, it's what's in your head that counts, and what you do is what you ought to be judged on. I don't put any stock in prejudice, and I have little tolerance for those who do.

That said, things are a little different in jail and in prison. It is a more brutal and primitive way of life. So, no matter how enlightened you are, racial gangs sort of form up, and when somebody the same color as you gets jumped, you jump in to help him. I'm not saying this is a great thing, but just so that you understand that's how it is in there.

So anyway, I knew this one racial group that had been vying for power before they brought me in was not happy that I was now the one running things. But despite not being happy, they were scared of me because my reputation preceded me. How could it not? I'd made it the point of my life to make sure that I was the baddest of the bad, the most lethal. I'd put the hurt on enough upstarts to ensure that these guys knew the only way to take me down was to rat-pack me – that's when you get jumped by a bunch of guys at once.

So, there I was up on the second tier overlooking a ten foot drop or so, and these dudes rushed me. One guy was on my neck, another guy had a hold of my arms, and then in front of me there was this guy who's just stabbing the crap out of me with a toothbrush. It was sharp enough to puncture me (most notably right above my eye and in my neck), but it was mostly blunt force trauma, so a lot of bruising. If that makes this sound better, it shouldn't. Getting stabbed with a butter knife is about the worst kind of stabbing there is.

So, these guys were just wearing me out, but down below there was someone in the day room, and he was the only guy in my tank the same color as me who wasn't a fish (somebody brand new to jail who doesn't know how things work). He saw what these guys were doing to me, and he knew that "you fight one, you fight all," so he rushed up the stairs. He got the one guy off of my neck, and the minute I could breathe again, I got the other guy off of my arm, and the guy who had been stabbing me tried to run. He made it all the way to his cell, but before he could lock himself in, I grabbed him by the shirt and pulled him out, then I gripped the back of his pants – and somehow during the melee he sailed over the railing for a nice ten-foot fall. Who knows who was responsible? I'm not saying that I did it, just that I happened to be nearby when he took his flying lessons.

And that was the end of that. The rest of the tank settled down, deciding that if three guys and a shank weren't good enough for taking me down, they'd be better off just falling in line.

Now, I want you to understand, I don't take a lot of

pride in this. I was a bad dude in a bad place, and these are the sorts of things that happened. In a very real way, this was all a consequence of that vow I made as a kid, and I want to show you, the reader, what happens when you follow these sorts of mindsets to their logical conclusions, because maybe you did something similar at some point in your life.

So, I got the tank settled down, the guy who stabbed me got hurt real bad, and nobody saw it. Everybody saw it, but nobody saw it, because that's the code. None of the inmates told the tale, and so the deputies did a skin search and knew I was involved, but they couldn't pinpoint exactly how I was involved. There was a guy smashed on the ground (he lived, don't worry) and me leaking from a bunch of holes in my chest and face and neck, but they didn't have any supporting details, so life went on.

At the time, it really didn't occur to me that I wouldn't need to constantly fight for my life if I would just live in an upstanding sort of way. Everyone's got their own level that they call rock bottom.

This wasn't the bottom for me yet. Not by a long shot.

# Chapter 6

I thought I was a motorcycle enthusiast. The feds said I was an outlaw biker. In retrospect, I suppose they were right.

I'd grown up in Oceanside with an early exposure to the Mescaleros and other biker gangs, and so as my criminal endeavors expanded, I spent more and more time around certain establishments. Without getting into too many details here, let's just say I was part of the wider 1% community.

Incidentally, you may have seen a patch on somebody's jacket that says "1%er" or heard the term. Basically, it means outlaw biker. It comes from when the American Motorcyclist Association, trying to distance themselves from criminal stereotypes for those who ride, said that "99% of motorcycle owners are law-abiding citizens." Organizations who did not feel the need to distance themselves from the assumption of criminality began referring to themselves as the 1%, meaning that they were not law-abiding citizens.

So, you may want to avoid crossing someone wearing a 1%er patch on their sleeve.

Anyway, ever since I saw Evil chasing his old lady through my yard as a kid, and I thought bikers were the toughest guys out there, I got closer and closer to their galaxy until I found myself in it. I stood at the nexus of three such galaxies: the underground martial arts community (basically UFC before the cameras, sponsors, and lawyers), the dark side of the Pacific Islander community, and the bikers in my area. I started making more money from my activities, I gained a fearsome reputation, and I felt invincible.

That's why I flew off the handle when someone ripped off my partner.

## Arizona Girls

You see, I didn't find any compelling reason to keep my day job, as collections and associated activities was paying so much better and gave an outlet to my angst. In fact, business was booming, so I expanded the scope of my enterprise. That meant finding some help, and the help came in the form of a guy we'll name "Tom."

I had fronted Tom a large stash of stuff because we were doing business together. Well, some cats from Arizona got it in their heads that it was a great idea to rip him off, and they stole it. I don't know if they knew about my involvement or not, but this was my business partner, and stealing from him was stealing from me. The value of goods and currency taken was about $40,000.

I was livid. The theft brought the old collections experience out of me, and I told Tom we had to do something about what had happened. That's how we ended up in my car speeding through the desert towards Phoenix, but unbeknownst to us, our eventual destination was prison.

We found out where these guys hung out, and two girls happened to be around, so we made the approach and got them out of there. The prosecutors referred to this part of the incident as "double kidnapping," but they weren't able to make that stick because of how we handled the situation. But I'm getting ahead of myself.

So, there we are, in Arizona, with these two girls who had close ties with the guys who had ripped us off. We figured having them gave us a sort of leverage for getting our stuff back. So what we did was we told these girls,

"Look, there's no sense in us being aggressive or mean to you two. Why should we tie you up, gag you, and find a basement somewhere? That sounds horrible. We just want our money. So, tell you what: If you promise not to make any calls or try and run back to your buddy out in Arizona, you can just hang out with us and we'll have a great time. We'll take you to Disneyland, Sea World, wherever, and you'll be as high as you care to be while we're doing it. Unlimited drugs."

As it happened, these two new female comrades were not exactly paragons of virtue, and doing a bunch of dope in the happiest place on earth while pretending to be kidnapped sounded like a great idea to them. They told us, "Let's party."

Our plan worked, sort of. We and the girls had a good old time running around California until those other guys paid up and we parted ways. The only problem was that someone had reported the two girls as kidnapped, so the FBI was suddenly involved and looking into us.

## Caught

I was driving one of these girls around Oceanside one day, when I started noticing quite a few unmarked vans in my neighborhood and an unusual number of Crown Victorias parked around. It doesn't take a genius to figure out who those leery dudes in sunglasses were. I dropped the girl off at a motel and watched as a parade of vehicles started up their engines to follow me.

It must have looked ridiculous, in hindsight. There I was in flip flops, shorts, and a Hawaiian shirt, driving my car, tailed by fifteen law enforcement vehicles – but they didn't turn their lights on. Apparently, this was an inter-departmental, multi-agency FBI task force dedicated to bringing me in, and the brief had made sure to tell everyone just how dangerous I was. So, I drove off to the freeway like a mama duck followed by her trail of ducklings.

I didn't find it at all funny at the time. I knew that I had a reputation. I knew that law enforcement had been waiting for their chance to come and get me. So, all that was going through my head as I changed lanes on the freeway and watched fifteen other cars do the same was, "How am I going to live long enough to see a trial?" I was going to go peacefully, I had decided a long time ago, but I wasn't about to surrender peacefully just to eat a bunch of lead and have a police report that said, "Oops." I waited until I was almost past the exit, then I pulled my steering wheel hard and exited, nearly causing a fifteen-car pile-up behind me as all of the other cars scrambled to follow me. I didn't wait to see how they managed. I floored it.

I sped off of the exit, took my turn, and stopped my car outside a nice café and restaurant that I knew of. I jumped out of my car and literally ran inside, to the middle of the dining area, and I turned around and stood there with my hands over my head. Law enforcement was only thirty seconds behind me or so, and I had a nice crowd of innocent bystanders around me ensuring that there weren't any "aggressive motions" on my part, if you get my drift.

So, I guess you could say this whole debacle was a learning experience. Mostly what I learned was that a S.W.A.T. team isn't gentle as they cuff you and throw your sorry butt in the back of a van. But things didn't go quite the way the feds anticipated either.

The kidnapping case was a real non-start once it came to light that when the girls got picked up, they were high in the sky and happy about it. They had never been bound or restrained, and they had spent the whole time going to the San Diego Zoo, meeting Mickey Mouse up in Anaheim, and generally having a grand old bacchanal. The prosecution's argument went down in flames, so they came to the negotiating table.

The prosecution asked me to plead guilty to a weapons charge. During the raid on my associate's place, they had found a sawed-off shotgun, which is illegal to own. Funny enough, it actually wasn't my gun, but the idea was plead guilty to that and they'd let the kidnapping charges go. Now, the kidnapping case was weak, but the stakes were high – you could do life in prison for a double kidnapping. So, I took the plea deal, said that the gun at my partner's house was mine, and I went in for my first felony charge and, subsequently, found out what a federal penitentiary was like.

Like I said, it was a learning experience.

# Chapter 7

Don't be a smart alec.

That's the first thing tangoing with federal prosecution taught me. Unfortunately, things would have gone better for me if I had adhered to that advice earlier.

You see, it wasn't enough that I'd done some minor stints in jail, had dangerous criminal associations, and was violent enough that they had sent an actual twenty-man S.W.A.T. team with police backup to make my arrest. Nope. I had to make sure "flight risk" was stamped on my record, too.

In my defense, I just thought I was playing a joke – and also playing peacock.

I was in the courthouse there in San Diego for the kidnapping charge, and I did not particularly like how the trial was going at that point nor how I was being treated. So, like any mature man would do, I filled my sandwich bag from lunch with water and I threw it at the marshal outside of my cell.

We called this "gassing," and at the time I thought it was a great laugh because of how it makes people panic. I just filled my bag with water, but you can imagine that sometimes guys fill them with *ahem* other things.

The marshal wasn't too happy with me, and in my youthful indignation, I felt that his response was disproportional to my little prank. They literally threw me in a new cell, alone, with no air flow or cellmates, but with plenty of swearing and threats. They tossed a wet blanket on my good time, and something the marshal said must have really rubbed me the wrong way. I should have just let it go at that, but my first joke demanded an encore.

Seeing as how the marshal thought he was pretty tough,

and the judge thought I wasn't worth listening to, and how everybody seemed to think that I was there at the court-house by anything other than my own good pleasure – I decided to show them. I went to the toilet and popped the cardboard center out of the toilet paper roll, folded it up just right, and made a lock slip. It worked like a charm, and the door of that cell came right open for me.

Just try to visualize the scene that happened next:

A proceeding is going on inside of a courtroom, complete with judge, jury, and defendants, and in walks little old me in an orange jumpsuit – in plain view. I walked across the court until I reached the marshal who had thrown me in the tank, and I tapped him on his shoulder while everyone watched, not quite sure what to do. The marshal turned around, and while his mouth was still hanging open at the shock of seeing me, I took my cardboard lock slip, tucked it in his shirt pocket behind his badge, patted it, and said, "Your security leaves much to be desired."

Now, in my head, this was sort of where things ended, with him dumbfounded at my ingenuity and sheer force of personality, and me with a satisfied grin on my face. Reality, however, didn't stop there, and the marshal's dumbfounded look turned to rage pretty fast. Seeing the signs of the times, I turned on my heels and split, only to hear the hollering and added footsteps of backup as all of these officers started chasing me.

I was never trying to escape, just trying to make the U.S. Marshall look like a fool, so I headed straight back to where I had been detained. I locked myself back into my cell before they could "re-capture" me, with all of the rough handling and "accidental contact" that would entail. To slow them down a bit, I bent the closing arm of the cell door down, wedging it in the entrance.

Good things come in threes, they say, but for me, apparently it's bad decisions. When they were finally able to catch up to me, and the posse rushed in to find me locked back in my cell, I thought it was a great idea to thumb my nose at them, stick out my tongue, and do a little dance. When they could not open the door due to the bent closing mechanism, they were furious.

I tell you what, I've never seen a broken door broken down so quickly.

So, despite the fact that I'd safely seen to my own recapture, the marshal and his buddies saw it fit to re-capture me for themselves – from inside of my cell. In layman's terms, they sent in the goon squad and beat the crap out of me. And then all I had for my pranks was a couple of cracked bones, plenty of bruises, and an "escape attempt" added to my file.

This actually is important to my story, however, because of the impact it had on my sentencing. Bumping up my security level one degree higher with that added stamp on my record sealed the deal for where they would send me: To the notorious maximum-security Federal Correctional Institution in El Reno, Oklahoma.

# Chapter 8

Maximum-security federal prison is not like jail.

There are no fish, for one thing. Everyone around you is quite experienced in the art of incarceration. Everyone's got their dirt, their hustle, their allies and their enemies. Everyone knows the rules and is committed to enforcing those rules.

You learn to be very polite in maximum-security federal prison, because every single person there is either already a killer, or quite capable of it. Sure, I was a tough enforcer and an exceptional fighter, but I still knew enough to be wary. It doesn't matter how good you are if five guys come at you at once, no matter what the movies say. Also, some of the corrections officers are quicker than others to resort to non-official correctional methods, if you get my drift. There was one correctional officer in particular, a red-headed hillbilly that took a disliking to me and enjoyed harassing me. But I'll get around to him later.

So, I learned to be polite, be on time, and make sure I had a good attitude, because the consequences were stiff around El Reno.

The company was more dangerous, too, and fool that I was, I liked it. I liked being thrown in with a more savage species of shark. I liked that my cellmate was a member of the Kansas City mob. I liked that the sort of bikers they sent here were from gangs that everyone knew across the country, across the world. I befriended these people, and it became my ambition to join this tougher biker gang that was represented there.

Still, life was strict. I had "martial arts expert" scrawled across my prisoner file, so whenever they had to move me, instead of just cuffs, I got handcuffs on my wrists and ankles, both of which were connected to a rigid iron bar between my legs. Not a lot you can do in that set-up, and remember, I had attempted to "escape" before. I guess this time the security did not "leave much to be desired."

Down time was a lot of chewing the fat, playing dominoes or pinochle, and pumping iron. It was a different time, the eighties. Civilian motorcycle clubs would actually come on the grounds of our maximum-security penitentiary and have carnivals from time to time. We had weightlifting competitions (at which I set a couple of records). I was the middleweight arm wrestling champion one year, and I got up to bench pressing four hundred pounds, which is not bad for a guy who's 5'9". And yes, there were bigger guys who could lift more weight – a lot of them, in fact. But as I like to say, the interesting thing about big guys is that they've been big their whole lives. They generally aren't used to being in real danger during a fight. Whereas me, on the other hand, had fought for my life nearly every day since I was a little kid dodging Dad's flashbacks and disapproval, and the associated beatings. There were a few scraps at El Reno, and my reputation continued to grow.

Being at this particular penitentiary was a turning point for me in more ways than one, and frankly, these ways were in opposite directions. On the one hand, I was a little older now, and having seen the disastrous consequences of my courtroom pranks, a little wiser as well. On the other hand, being around the particular bikers I met in El Reno also represented what you might call an escalation in my criminal career.

But in the meantime, I was in prison, and there were no fishes here.

## The Riot and Its Consequences

You'll recall from an earlier chapter that I told you about the racial politics of prison life. Basically, the rule is "if you fight one, you fight all," and in jail this may not always be such a big deal, on account of so many individuals being on short terms or misdemeanors and not really wanting to get involved in a brawl.

Here at El Reno, however, everyone knew the rules, and everyone was committed. This was no one's first rodeo, so on the fateful day that some guy from Racial Group A ticked off somebody from Racial Group B, and Racial Group C had an opinion about it… it was all hands on deck. Back in county jail, when I got jumped by those three guys, one other guy jumped in to help me, bringing the total to five belligerents. Here at the riot, no one was on the sideline, so a personal beef quickly turned to a cell-block-wide race brawl.

It's a shameful thing, really, but that day, no matter what your politics were, you were fighting for your skin. I got some marks on me – a couple of stab wounds and some bruises – and usually that wouldn't have been too big of a deal once they finally settled everyone down, but a couple of inmates had died in the rumble, and there was hell to pay.

In those days, there were no real security cameras in prison, and certainly not one on every corner like today. There was no panic button that would usher all the inmates into their cells for a lockdown. It was all analog back then, and that meant at the end of a brawl they did a skin search to find out who was involved, and who they could pin the results on.

Never mind the fact that if you find a guy with a slash across his chest, that doesn't tell you if he was fighting or just in the wrong place at the wrong time, but I guess there I go contradicting myself, because everyone was involved that day. The corrections officers just had no way of knowing who exactly did what, and none of the inmates were going to tell them.

So, to account for the calls for punishment in relation to the couple of guys who ended up dead, everyone who was found with marks on him was assumed to be involved and sent into solitary confinement, including me.

I didn't think the old SHU program would be so bad for me, but something happened during that time that still haunts me to this day.

# Chapter 9

On the inside, they call solitary confinement the "SHU program" (pronounced like "shoe") because of the acronym for its official name: Segregated Housing Units. I ended up doing eighteen months.

When I told this story one time, the gentleman I was speaking with asked me over what length of time I did this eighteen months of solitary. I told him that I did it in eighteen months, which surprised him, because that sort of treatment isn't legal in this country any longer. Back then it was. And today, inmates in solitary get one hour of sunshine a day to break up the monotony of the dimly lit isolation chamber. Back then it was one hour a week.

I wasn't assigned to eighteen months of solitary at first, though. I was assigned a year, in keeping with my involvement in the brawl where I'd been unlucky enough to get tagged. But something happened nine months in that made them decide to extend my internship in the SHU program.

**The Chess Incident**

It's easy to think abstractly about solitary confinement and worry about its deep psychological effects, neurosis, etc., but the reality of it is that boredom is your first enemy to do battle with. There is nothing quite so mind-numbing and tedious as staying in a tiny concrete box for twenty-four hours a day with no outside view to look at, no one to talk to, no responsibilities, and no plans. The tedium literally drives people insane, and life in solitary is a delicate balance of staying on the level. So, when you find yourself left in isolation for an extended period of time, you need a strategy for getting through it with your mind in one piece.

I came up with something that worked pretty well, though – for a while, at least.

They'd provide me with those miniature hotel soaps so I could wash myself, and I took to collecting them and carving them into chess pieces using a short pencil. I drew a chess board on the floor of the cell, and over time I had carved all thirty-two pieces to set out and play. I didn't have a partner, of course, so I played myself. It worked for me. It was like a puzzle, trying to outdo my plans on white's side, then flipping it around and trying to break through with black's side, and then switching back again. I was good at chess, a keen student of the game, so in my mind, there were worse things than some externally imposed time to become a grandmaster. At least that's how I felt during high times. During low points, at least it was something to do.

I became obsessive. I didn't really have much other choice, and it made the waiting bearable. I did chess problems, played games, analyzed my successes and my failures. Chess became my whole world, my salvation, my escape, and the freedom in my mind.

My spirits were in okay shape, then. I'd take breaks when meals came, wash up, take naps and all that, but chess was the constant thing tying it all together and giving my time meaning. Then, once a week, the officers would show up to cuff me, unlock my cell, and walk me outside for an hour of sunshine by myself. They would use that time, naturally, to check my cell to make sure I wasn't pulling a Shawshank and tunneling through the walls or anything like that. Then, I'd come back, and for another 167 hours the four walls and my little army of soap chess pieces were my only companions.

One day, a certain guard whom I held in low esteem and who particularly hated me, got assigned to my unit. He's the guy I mentioned in a previous chapter –

redheaded, hillbilly, and arrogant. He hated Californians, bikers, and guys who thought they were tough, which was three strikes for me. On this day, however, I wasn't going to let him get in my head. I had a good game of chess going, trying out some different openings, and I was looking forward to seeing the sun and the sky for my weekly hour. You can't imagine how much you look forward to going outside when it's only an hour a week.

So, I went out and got my sunshine, then got taken back through the halls of the old dungeon back to my cell, where they unlocked my feet, removed the bar between my legs, and then sent me in with my handcuffs still on so they could lock the door before taking my cuffs off through the pie slot. The redhead seemed pleased with himself, but I didn't care what was going through that empty head of his.

Then, suddenly, I did care what was going through his head. When the door closed behind me, I looked at the floor and saw every one of my intricately carved chess pieces ground into powder. My board was littered with the remnants of soap, and my one way of keeping a check on my mind was gone. My safety, my defiance, my entire world was gone.

I hated then like I had never hated anyone or anything ever before, but I wore it with a cold, icy control. I turned around, glaring, only to see the hillbilly guard nod his chin at the massacred chess army and say, "Tough s***." Then, he spat his tobacco chaw on the ground in my cell, and any doubt that he had been the one behind it was removed.

I calmly raised my hands and put them through the slot, where the cocky guard undid my cuffs, and then I rolled my wrists around, grabbed him by the forearm, and fell back.

His face smashed into the heavy metal doors, and in his panic, he must have pushed away with his legs, because I was lifted off the ground, but this was part of my plan. As soon as I had a foot or so of room, I rowed hard with my legs and sat down again, smashing his head into the metal. There was a lot of shouting, then, and I couldn't see any of it from inside my cell, I just felt my hands locked in a death grip around this monster's arm, and every time they'd pull him back, I'd row back again and crash his bloody face into the door.

His entire arm and shoulder were through that little slot. He must have dislocated it, but I didn't let up. I wore him out, letting some slack go, then busting his head, then letting some slack go, then busting him over and over and over. I broke the orbital socket of his skull and plenty of other places on his face. It'd be tiresome to list all of his injuries here. But my mind was like a rock – dull, unresponsive, one all-consuming substance, and that was rage. I wasn't letting go of this jerk for anybody.

It took a firehose to finally break my grip. They sprayed me down something fierce, and then they rushed him off to get medical attention, I suppose. But as for me, not for the first time in my life, they sent in the goon squad.

They beat the living daylights out of me. They made sure that I got it every bit as bad as I'd given it, and then some. They broke my ribs, stomped on my hands, kicked me in the head, over and over. Five of them punished me to the edge of being beaten to death.

And yet all I could think about was that my chessboard was gone, taken in a fit of childish spite.

## Fallout

The beating, while painful, traumatic, and crippling, actually served me well in one way, and badly in another. They couldn't report what had happened between me and old Red because then they would have to explain about beating me within an inch of my life. (In case you're wondering, no, it isn't legal to stomp on a prisoner's head long after he's been subdued.) So that meant I was off the hook for what certainly would have been attempted murder charges, but it also meant I was off the hook for medical attention, because again, they would have had to explain.

So, clinging to life, I didn't get to go to the infirmary; they just extended my solitary to eighteen months, and the last nine were quite a bit worse than the first. I still can't think about it without getting emotional at the barbarism of it all. They literally chained me to a raised concrete block in what we call a box car, doped me up on Thorzine, and left me broken and babbling to myself for nine months. This, in the United States of America.

The guard I wore out lived and came back to work, but only in the gun towers. It's accepted practice that when a guard gets attacked like he did, that he doesn't go back into the general population. The higher-ups know enough to realize that they've probably done something below the belt for an inmate to be willing to accept the consequences of assaulting an officer in prison. As for me, I rode out the rest of my time in the SHU program delirious, dazed, and in excruciating pain.

This wasn't rock bottom for me yet, but believe me – it was close.

Incidentally, and this will never be official because of how the correctional officers responded, but this event is what triggered a change in protocol when transferring an inmate to his cell. Today, prisoners have to stand facing away from the pie slot and put their hands in backwards to get their cuffs off. No sense in having somebody repeat my trick.

# Chapter 10

Things had begun to spiral out of control. I just didn't know it yet.

To me, I was getting my wish! Even with all of the nonsense that happened to me in El Reno, I figured that the institutional revolving door of prison was just part of the life I chose. The important thing was the introductions I'd made to this bigger and badder biker gang. I earned many of my stripes on the inside, and by the time I got out, I was in a good position to join up.

By my calculations, that made me bigger and badder, or at least it was recognition of how tough I knew I was.

I was accepted into the organization, and I continued on with my prolific life of crime, completely unaware that an entire government task force was working around the clock to bring me down.

Here's how it happened.

I'd been out of El Reno for less than a year when I caught an assault beef. They picked me up for attempted murder and assault and battery with intent of great bodily harm, for which I was given some state time in the California Department of Corrections. I went and served my sentence, and it wasn't so bad, but when I was about a week away from being released, the carefree days came to an end. I was giving away my stuff, getting ready to be done with the CDC, when they came to my cell, slapped cuffs on me, and told me I was being indicted.

For what?

Conspiracy.

Never mind the fact that I'd been in prison for five of the six years they were trying to prosecute me for supposedly running a criminal conspiracy. My sorry butt got thrown on a Con Air flight and transferred to the Metropolitan Correctional Center in San Diego.

I called my girlfriend and told her what was going on. I couldn't believe what they were trying with me, but I could have saved my breath. My girlfriend told me it was all over the news: Marcel Becker indicted for racketeering and conspiracy along with other members of a certain biker gang. I still have the news clippings, in fact. It was odd to see my name in the papers so often, and in this case for something I hadn't done.

Being innocent was a new experience. I wasn't sure I liked it yet.

Still, I figured that I had a great shot at beating the rap on this "systematized production and distribution of methamphetamine" that I was being accused of, mainly because I didn't do it. Turns out that wasn't quite enough for the feds. They were mad at me. I'd gotten off on big crimes that they knew I'd done but couldn't stick me with any real time for. One way or another, I was going down for this one – guilty or not.

I wasn't amenable to that line of reasoning, however. I had every intention of getting off scot-free.

Here is the entirety of my involvement in the criminal conspiracy I was alleged to have coordinated:

There was a guy in my motorcycle club that we'll just call "Briggs." He was a mess – the sort of guy who never had a running car or a running bike, so he asked me for a lift to the weekly meeting one time, and I said, "Yeah." And on the way he said, "Can make a stop? There's this guy that keeps ditching me, and I want to see if I can hook up with him. It's on the way." So I said, "Yeah, okay. Fine."

We pulled into this guy's house, and lo and behold, he just happened to be home. So he invited us in, and then Briggs said, "Hey Flash, I need to talk to this dude for a minute. You mind?" And I said, "No." I sat down in the living room and started watching *The Price Is Right* on the TV, and then they went in the back for five, maybe ten minutes tops. When they came out, the guy we came to see was leaking a little bit – puffed lips, a little blood from his nose – but he wasn't hurt bad. The two of them were walking arm in arm, so I figured that whatever issue they had, they'd arrived at an equitable resolution. So we got up and left.

That was all that they had. I look like a real mastermind in this one, right?

Turns out Briggs was a high-level guy in the meth conspiracy charges. Oh, and the guy who got beat up? He was an informant for the federal government. Apparently, he told the justice department, "Hey, I'll give you as many of these guys from this particular biker club as I can get." So, every guy this clown had ever met was getting pulled up on charges, many of them very flimsy. He tried to smut up and gin up charges against everyone, even if he didn't really have any evidence or hard information.

This is what had me looking at twenty-seven to life for criminal conspiracy. I was with Briggs when he stopped by to beat up another guy – even though by everyone's admission, I was in the other room watching *The Price Is Right*, with no idea what was going on in the other room. I couldn't even hear them.

"Circumstantial" is a good word for this type of evidence. Also, "unconvincing," "inconclusive," and "nothing burger."

This, in my opinion, was a wholly manufactured business. At one point in court, the prosecutor said, "Your Honor, this is one of the most brilliant criminal minds to have ever associated with this organization, and he is lethal." There's another bail enhancement, just by saying that stuff. So anyhow, they were trying to lock me up for a long time. They were going to do anything they could.

First, the judge looked at the evidence compiled against me and decided that they would separate my case from the others and try me first. Some of the other guys would get convicted for this, without question, but the evidence against me was extremely weak. Again, this was largely due to the fact that I wasn't guilty.

As the weeks dragged on, it became clear to everybody that the effort to get Marcel Becker was falling apart. The other side came to the negotiating table, but they weren't in a gracious mood. Their first offer was strict, and I said no. Their next offer might have sounded tempting – if I had been a complete airhead. They wanted me to plead guilty to a "no-time felony" where I'd be convicted for a felony, but there would be no jail time on the plea. Sounds great, right? Except for the little detail that California had recently passed its Three Strikes law. I had enough strikes on my record by this time that a single new one would have qualified me instantly for twenty-five to life. So, in their minds, they were hoping I'd sign the "no-time" deal, I'd be released, and then as soon as I'd crossed the street, they would have been able to arrest me and prosecute me under the Three Strikes statute.

I'm not stupid, I just look like this. They thought I had figured out how to coordinate an entire criminal enterprise from inside prison (harder in real life than in the movies), but they expected me to fall for their lame traps. Not on my watch.

So, after negotiating down and down, they came back with one last plea deal before we went to trial: Plead guilty to a misdemeanor possession charge of one dose of meth.

I didn't want to do it. I told my attorney, "We've got to fight this all the way! This is the one time in my life I'm actually not guilty of what they're trying to get me on." My lawyer, in his great wisdom, painted me a different sort of picture than the one I had in my mind.

He said, "Flash, listen. I know the evidence is weak. You know the evidence is weak. Heck, even the judge knows it. But they're going to stack the jury with a bunch of blue-haired ladies from Coronado, and the prosecution is going to walk in front of them and assassinate your character. They will bring up every dirty deed you've ever done – and that part will be true, Flash. You think the evidence in this particular occasion is going to matter to them after that? Going to trial is too risky. Take the deal."

When he put it that way, my righteous indignation faded somewhat. I took the deal. I wish that was where the story ended, but it's not.

I was sentenced to one year on this misdemeanor charge I'd pled guilty to. Then, the federal bureau of prisons handed down their decision on what institution I'd do my time in: Federal Correctional Institution La Tuna in Texas, also known as, "The place we are sending you for a violent, bloody death." See, this is how the federal bureau of prisons works: They understand that criminal affiliations have certain realities attached to them, so generally they try and A) get you as far from the home base of your criminal organization as possible, which was why they sent a San Diego boy to Oklahoma the first time, and B) depending on the organization, they either try to scatter you around as much as possible or, more commonly, they stick you all in the same joint so that they can keep an eye on you. El Reno was where they sent all of the members of the biker gang I was in. La Tuna was where they sent our rival gang.

They knew this. They did this on purpose. They couldn't get me in court, so they sent me to La Tuna to die.

# Chapter 11

There isn't much of an upside when the government sends you to an unofficial death sentence.

I was headed to La Tuna, home of our rival gang, and there was no love lost between us. I'm keeping the names vague on purpose, but understand how this shakes out: A lot of biker gangs are officially enemies on the street, but once you get in jail, it's understood that all of that should be laid aside. After all, we've got a common enemy on the inside: the guys with sniper rifles in the guard towers. So generally, even enemies get along okay in prison.

That was not the case with our rival gang. We were sworn enemies. Any time they saw us, they were honor-bound to try and hurt, maim, or kill us, and that didn't change in prison – their prison.

Never mind the fact that the mere reality of the feds being willing to do such a thing raised a lot of questions. This is how mad they were at me. This is how badly they wanted to get me. They weren't going to let me go to jail, then get back out and do my old tricks anymore. The game had changed.

But I couldn't think about that when I landed in La Tuna. I had to survive first.

It's a blur now, but back then the time passed at a snail's pace. You ever feel like it's you against the world? In there, it was. Every eye was on me when my back was turned, every shiv had my name on it. I had to be on high alert every moment of every day if I was going to have any chance of getting out alive.

The first time I got jumped, I'd barely had time to settle in. Five bikers with improvised weapons jumped me in the yard, stabbing me like a pin cushion. I fought like a wounded animal, taking plenty of hits but giving them too. I lasted long enough for the guards to find us, subdue us, and then do a skin check. Well, the skin check showed Mr. Becker with numerous stab wounds, so they decided he was "involved." That mean the SHU program, or solitary confinement, for a month or so. Then, once that time was up, I was on high alert again, because it was only a matter of time before I'd get jumped again.

They were afraid of me. They had a healthy respect for my abilities that meant they'd send four or five guys to carry out an attack. I was the guy that everyone feared, just like I'd always wanted, but it turns out that doesn't stop people from wanting you dead.

This was my entire year: Get jumped and stabbed by a numerically superior force intent on murdering me, last long enough to get thrown into solitary confinement, get released back into the prison's general population again, then repeat. My martial arts training saved my life over and over. If I hadn't been a fighter, I would have died several times over.

On one of many such occasions when I was jumped and rat-packed by a bunch of guys, the guards got involved in a way that added insult to injury. It also added injury to injury. A cop in the gun tower shot me in my right hip with a block gun.

For those of you who aren't familiar, correctional officers often use "non-lethal" ammunition to pacify riots and such in prisons. Today, this is done with a certain level of sophistication. They generally use beanbags or baton rounds filled with foam that are drag or fin stabilized, and they can fill these with anything from chemical agents to marking dyes. In years past, they used rubber bullets. Well, in my day they used block guns that just shot wood.

Imagine a block of wood hurtling through the air with

the force of an explosion behind it. Well, not only did this gunshot take my legs out from under me, it also began a slow degenerative condition called avascular necrosis.

Getting shot is never fun, but being shot by the guy who's supposed to be enforcing justice while you're fighting for your life in an ambush? That's just the pits.

## Better Days

Sometimes during the course of my criminal career, my jail and prison stays had been downright pleasant. Heck, I had friends in prison, and when I didn't, I made new ones. One time I shared a cell with Jeff Boguskie, who was known as "Sinner." We both lived in the same Lakeside apartment complex, we traveled in the same circles, and we hung with the same group of bikers. He was a shot-caller like me, a well-respected, high-ranking convict. We wound up in the same cell when he was tank captain in the El Cajon jail. We had fun and laughed so much my stomach hurt. We even had one of the guards that would give us a few cigarettes after lockdown every night. That term was a barrel of laughs, some of the best days of my life up till that point. To this day, we remain best friends, and we often vacation together.

On two occasions, I shared a cell with a neat guy named David Barron. And sure, he had his faults – namely his occupation as a sicario for the Arellano Felix Cartel – but I tell you, he was a great guy to hang out with. When I was in El Reno, I shared a cell with an old-time gangster from the Kansas City Mob named Lindsey Pearson. In a lot of ways, he taught me how to be a convict on the inside and sort of took me under his wing. I remember one time I was laying on my cot in the cell, listening to music with headphones on a Walkman. I was singing and having a grand old time writing a letter or doing whatever I was doing, when Lindsey got my attention like he had something important to tell me. He was always big on teachable moments, so I took my headphones off and listened.

"You know, Flash," he said, "let me tell you something. When I was younger, all I wanted to be able to do was sing. I even tried to get my mom to hook me up with singing lessons or get me into a choir, because all I ever wanted to do was to be able to become a singer and a performer. I just really wanted to sing. It's all I wished for as a child."

He shifted his weight and looked thoughtful.

I said, "Really?"

He said, "Yeah. You know what I wish for now?" I sensed a life lesson coming. "I wish you could sing," he said.

He got me good. He was like that, though – a dry sense of humor. He was a tough old gangster, and I enjoyed spending time with him.

A lot of my stays in prison were just fine by me.

But this current sentence was different. This sentence was hell. Being in La Tuna reminded me of being strapped to a concrete block, doped up on Thorzine. There was nothing I could do but wait out the time and hope I stayed alive.

Against the odds, I outlasted them. I got my $200 and personal effects, and I was deposited back out on the streets on Friday the 13th of December. I boarded a plane and returned to San Diego on flight 911 to a scene that had completely changed.

# Chapter 12

I had reached the status of public enemy number one.

That much was clear to me. When I got out of La Tuna at the end of 1991, I had a nagging feeling that perhaps things could not continue as they once had before. I sat down and did some thinking:

First of all, the FBI had an entire multi-agency task force dedicated to yours truly. People were on the lookout for any excuse to snatch me up, and once in their hands, I could be sent back to La Tuna for round two of unofficial execution. I doubted that I'd live through that again. The feds were so mad at me that they were willing to cross lines in order to get me off the street. That thin blue line was trained on my forehead like a laser sight.

Secondly, not only had the laws of the Golden State changed, federal criminal statutes had changed as well. First was the institution of mandatory minimum sentencing requirements, which ensured that my days of getting off easy because I had a good lawyer were through. If I got picked up for drug charges (or for something worse), there would be no slap on the wrist. There were mandatory minimums for time to be served, and they were harsh minimums. A lot of judges resigned over this law, in fact, because it took away their discretion. I wasn't a fan, but it was the new normal. That was the federal law. Added to this was the Three Strikes law in California that basically meant if I got picked up again, I would spend the rest of my life in prison – and they don't let you ride Harleys in there. I had no problem with the revolving door, but being a lifer? That was something else entirely.

So, there I was thinking that the landscape had perhaps changed, wondering how I'd gotten myself into such a predicament, when the last piece of the puzzle slid into place.

## The Drop-Off

I was fresh out, having only been released from prison for about two weeks. I was living at my girlfriend's apartment in Lakeside – and for those of you unfamiliar with San Diego geography, this is not a ritzy town on the shores of a lake. It's a semi-rough spot with lots of bars and gangs. I was still trying to wrap my head around what I was going to do with myself now that the feds were so thoroughly breathing down my neck, when I heard a knock at the door.

My girlfriend answered it, and a second later I heard her holler at me, "Flash! You gotta come deal with this."

My natural inclination was to think there would be another shot-caller from my biker gang at the door, or maybe a parole officer. Might even have been an old enemy with a score to settle, but when I got to the door, I saw two little kids: a boy and a girl.

They were my children, and behind them was my meth head ex-wife, smoking impatiently.

Before I could even get words out of my open mouth, the ex-wife said her piece:

"How are you? Good. So, I've had these brats the last six years while you were playing jailbird. Now it's your turn."

Then she left. Just went to the stairs and walked away. I shouted after her, of course. She didn't want to hear it. She was leaving them with me or she was leaving them on a street corner. As I watched from the balcony, her car pulled past, and I was out of words. The red lights on the back of her beat-up car faded, and I looked at those two kids standing there, embarrassed, a little cold, and lost.

"Go inside," I said. "My girlfriend'll – go meet the nice lady inside."

I looked back into the night again, completely at a loss. Even when I think about that day now, I'm just as flabbergasted as I was in the moment. I had no plan, no job, and no clue what I was going to do.

I didn't know how to be a civilian, much less a parent. My ex was a drug addict and in no mood to suffer rivals to her addiction. Besides that, she was gone, and I knew I'd never see her again. All of my family, by this time, was in Europe (as you might recall, we were immigrants). As I leaned against the wall outside and tried to get my bearing, suddenly I saw a picture of my life with some clarity: I was living with a stripper, I was a five-time felon, the feds wanted me to die, the criminal organization I was part of had opinions about people just bowing out, and suddenly I was an instant dad.

These kids had nothing. If I went to prison or abandoned them, I knew what would happen. They would become wards of the state, and I couldn't let that happen.

"I'll never be afraid of anybody," was my vow for my life. Fat lot of good it had done me. I had spent the last fourteen years either in prison or trying to get there. Suddenly the math had changed. I needed to go straight for these kids. It seemed like an impossibility, but it was the only option I could reconcile in my mind.

This marks a change in my life, and the second vow that ruled me: I will find a way to go straight for these kids.

# Chapter 13

When you're in deep with a criminal organization, you can't just say, "Well, fellas, it's been fun. Have a nice day."

In a lot of the street gangs, you hear them say things like "Blood in, blood out," meaning you get jumped in for your initiation (all the members beat you up). Then, they say "the only way out is in a box," meaning you're in the gang for life. Death is the only escape. This, however, is not how more sophisticated organizations do things.

When you're a "motorcycle enthusiast" like I was, there are only three ways of getting out: Out good, out bad, and out dead. I was aiming for door number one.

With "out good," the organization needs to be convinced that you have a legitimate reason for changing your lifestyle. If they agree to release you on good terms, you basically just walk down the road and move onto a new life. It's sort of like an honorable discharge from the military. "Out bad" is a little bit different. This is generally for people who have embarrassed the club in some way. Think of it like a dishonorable discharge, only instead of stripping you of your benefits, they tear the tattoos off of your body. At least you live, even if it's in shame and with a fair bit of looking over your shoulder in the future. And with "out dead," I imagine you can fill in the details.

Now, I'm not speaking specifically of the organization I was involved with, only of 1%er clubs in general that have been known to do these sorts of things, but it'll give you a picture of where I was at. Before I could go any further trying to straighten out for my kids, I had to break formal bonds with the criminal organization I had so fervently pursued all those years.

On the plus side, as an organization with an honor

code, biker gangs generally appreciate you being upfront with them about major life changes. After all, they don't want to get into a gun battle with you next to them only to find out that you've been toying with the idea of pacifism. That's not a guarantee that you'll be let out good, but it helps.

So, after preparing my case and going through the process, the biker organization understood why I had to make a change. After all, even there it was well understood that if you can't care for the most vulnerable in society (kids), then you can't really be trusted to care for the club either. You have to be a team player to succeed as a 1%er.

Besides that, it was understood that I had demonstrated my loyalty. I'd been leaned on by prosecutors to flip on my organization and fellow bikers in exchange for a deal, but I never said a word. I think the main reason I was let out good is because this aspect of my character was not in doubt. Today, in a different frame of mind, I cannot endorse or agree with much of what went on inside the gang, but I will never, ever speak a word to do harm to people I once called my brothers. That's just how I am.

So, there's the conundrum of criminal organizations – it may be criminal, but at least it's organized. This is a difficult point to make without seeming to wink at the dark side of the law, so let me be clear: Don't join a biker gang. I recommend you do something else with your time. We all ought to follow the law and steer clear of people and organizations that make a practice of violating it. However, in this mixed up, backwards, strange world we live in, sometimes blessings come in awfully strange packages. Here's what I mean: I learned teamwork in the gang. I made a few lifelong friends. I learned to put the organization's well-being above my own, a mindset that would serve me well in business later. And crucially, though there are a lot of drugs around these biker gangs, it is a generally accepted rule that there will be absolutely no intravenous injection of drugs among its members, and though drug use was allowed, it had to be in some sort of moderation. If it became a problem or ruled you, you were unreliable, and you were out bad.

Truthfully, I think the biker organization is the only reason I never ended up in the gutter, twitching and talking to myself.

Like I said, blessings come in strange packages.

## Now What?

So I got a pass. It was "out good" from the biker gang, but in many ways, I was worse off than before. All of the connections I'd worked to create since my teenage years were on the wrong side of the law. My money was running out, and I had to find work that didn't involve my old dirt.

My first opportunity, interestingly enough, came from my old cellmate David Barron, the assassin for the Arellano Felix cartel. Doesn't sound so legitimate, does it? Yet it was an improvement on my previous activities.

David had made a lot of money from his criminal enterprises, and there were some kids down in National City with a rap group called "Aztec Pride" that he had taken under his wing. He'd buy them matching outfits to perform in, cart them around in limousines, and take them to parties. He was bored, I think, and he got a kick out of promoting these teens and making the whole affair seem like a world-famous musical entourage. Well anyway, he needed a bodyguard for these guys, and bodyguarding is legal.

So I went down on our side of the border and rode around with these guys for a few days. The pay was good –

a little too good, actually. David was paying me five times what security work was worth, and I started wondering if this was just out of the goodness of his heart to help me out, or if he was trying to get his hooks into me. You know, sort of a "Hey, the cartel needs a service from you. You don't want to do it? What about all that money I've been paying you so you could play nice with your parole officer and take care of your kids? You owe me, Vato."

I wasn't quite on the dark side of society, but I was in no-man's land for sure. After two weekends, and getting paid five grand, I decided I needed to find a different gig.

David and I parted on friendly terms, and still with no idea what I was going to do, I at least had enough money to stall for a little while. I didn't want to do work that could end up dragging me back into my not-so-old way of life.

Incidentally, David passed away just a few years after this. It was 1997, and he was gunned down while attempting to assassinate a Mexican journalist who had been reporting on the cartel's activities. He was thirty-four years old. Those who live by the sword die by it, as I would see over and over among my friends as time went on.

# Chapter 14

I was not used to having no income.

In my former life, I had been well-compensated, and now, without a whole lot of legitimate connections, I looked around that apartment on Winter Gardens shaking my head. I had to provide for these kids somehow, and also, I didn't look so good to my parole officer if I was unemployed. My probation had stipulations, after all, and they could take it back.

A guy at the apartment complex kept telling me that they were hiring down at the docks, and I tried with all of my heart to do anything but that. It's a cliché, right? Ex-con gets a job loading boxes on ships or something. The pay was bad, the commute was bad, and I didn't want to do it.

My tune changed a bit once I exhausted every avenue I could think of.

No one would hire me. I was an ex-con, with tattoos and ties to powerful criminal organizations. It felt like I had the scarlet letter spray-painted on top of my shirt.

They say that every sentence is a life sentence, because for the rest of your life, you've got to explain why you have a record. This is the reason, I think, that so many people get caught up in the cycle of crime. They feel like it isn't worth trying to go legit, or maybe they try for a little while, but they make less money washing cars then they did dealing dope, and thinking nothing can change, they get back into their old dirt.

Well, that wasn't an option for me, but it still was no walk in the park. I had an extensive record, and no amount of pleading, charming, or negotiating would budge anyone. It was like I'd moved into a foreign country. All of the skills and tools that I'd been developing for the last decade were suddenly... useless. They didn't apply. I was thirty with the resume of a sixteen-year-old kid.

It felt like I had a dark cloud of doom hovering over my head.

So, with heavy feet, I marched down to the docks and asked if I could have a job.

## The Docks

$5.50 an hour.

That's what I was paid – minimum wage at the time, for my services as a laborer/firewatch at a maritime ship repair company. I'm not going to sit here and write that the "hours were long." Heck, I was desperate for long hours. Forty hours a week at $5.50 was not enough to take care of a household.

So, the work was legit, if the compensation was unlivable and the position unglamorous. But while I was not terribly concerned with how cool my job was; I was concerned with making enough money to stay afloat. Drifting back into the old life was always a temptation, and I knew I had to stay away, because you never know how strong your conviction is, right? So I made some decisions.

The first was that I got a side gig. It wasn't ideal. The only thing I could find was bouncing a strip club Friday and Saturday nights. It wasn't going to get me arrested because it wasn't illegal, but I knew it wasn't a place to stay at a moment longer than I needed to. See, suppose that hypothetically I used to be involved in a protection racket for this same strip club back when I had been in organized crime. Now I was working the door, and that's sort of a gray area because it wouldn't take much for an old contact to wander up and offer me something more lucrative than bouncing.

But I was desperate, and it had the double benefit of closing the gap on what I needed to make a living while not being technically illegal.

I had to cut ties with my best friend, Ron, the guy I used to get paired up with a lot in the biker organization I had just quit. I went to see him to explain the situation and said, "Ron, I love you like a brother, but I can't be around you while you're still in the mix." And to his credit, he understood. He didn't give me any flack, he just said, "You've got to do what you've got to do. See you when I see you."

It was just like the situation with David's rap group, and the situation at the strip club that I knew I would soon have to get out of. You walk in that twilight too long, and your conviction is going to waver. If you keep going in that barber shop, eventually you're going to get a haircut.

So, it was lonely, foreign, odd. Working at the docks, I didn't know anybody. I'd cut out all of my old friends. I was making peanuts. I thought that one of the ways I could help create some stability for these kids of mine that had shown up was to marry the woman I was living with. Turns out "marrying the stripper" is an actual cliché for making a bad decision, and it was.

Putting down the life of crime and edging away from the drugs was my thing, and my stripper/wife was none too enthused with my recent decisions. In my world we say, "She wasn't ready to put it down yet." She was still more than content to live in her addictions and revel in the criminal element. So when I started making these changes, she was not happy with me, to put it mildly. "So, first you go soft, throw away your reputation, quit bringing me dope, and now, what, you want me to be a mom?"

Home life was not bliss.

But there are two options in life: To accept conditions

as they exist, or to accept the responsibility for changing them. I was determined. I was trying my best. The road from sinner to saint was not a straight path for me, and boy was it muddy at times. But to say that I struggled is to say that I was alive and kicking. You only struggle when you're fighting against something.

That's nothing to be ashamed of, in my book.

# Chapter 15

The docks do not attract the crème de la crème of society.

Especially not in those days. It was the twilight zone, the in-between of productive society and its criminal underbelly. A lot of the guys were on drugs, most drank heavily, and plenty were involved in the sorts of biker gangs I was now out of. Parts of it felt all too familiar.

The docks were purgatory, the fence top, and any guy down there could go either way as far as life choices went.

There I was with a family to provide for, so I didn't care about the social hierarchy among peons or the gossip about who was joining up with what motorcycle club. I was out there hustling to try and be enough of an asset to keep my job and hopefully get a raise or a promotion. That's when I first started to learn that anytime you try and do something right, you're going to have what I affectionately refer to as "critics."

These were the guys who thought I'd become a push-over just because I'd left my place of prominence in the criminal underworld. Evidently, they took my change in lifestyle to mean that I'd been neutered, for all the smack talk and practical trouble they caused me.

Now, like when I described some of the things that happened in jail, I'm not particularly proud of this, but you have to understand the rules of where I found myself day in and day out. It was a more primitive sector of society at the time, let's say. So just like in my old days as a tank captain, I found that there were occasions when I would need to invite an individual to step into the boiler room with me and remind them that I hadn't lost any nerve. The only reason that their teeth remained in their mouths because I allowed them to remain there. I guess that people saw me trying to do right and they thought that I'd forgotten how to introduce someone to the floor.

Well, they thought wrong. I didn't seek out any trouble, but when it came I ensured that it only had a short tenure. Maybe this isn't the best method, but it's what I did, and I don't intend to sugarcoat this accounting of my life's turn-around.

Making a change was hard. It was frustrating at times, because there were lines I couldn't cross. I felt isolated, like I didn't have any brothers-at-arms anymore, no wingmen, and nobody to back me up.

Thank goodness for Tom Wright.

## First and Foreman

The sort of work we did at that company was essentially construction in dry docks on damaged or worn boats. If you just imagined a little fishing dingy, imagine something quite a bit bigger. I started out as a laborer, then was transferred to the facilities department, and I think my official title must have been "Assistant Boot-licker" at the time. I hadn't made "Boot-licker" yet. I was at the bottom of the ladder, but there was a foreman in charge of my team named Tom Wright, and he was a stand-up guy to me.

Tom worked hard and was fair. He wore a beard and was fairly tall – something like 6'1" I'd guess. He was rough and tumble, high mileage and hard living, but he didn't try to push me around or give me any guff I didn't deserve. We understood each other, kindred spirits in a way, and we became friends over time. We figured out that we lived near one another, so we actually started carpooling to work every day. I didn't think about it this way at the time, but it really was helpful knowing somebody where I worked and knowing that he had my back.

I learned a lot from Tom, a little about the trade and a bit more about life. He was a family man, the first such I'd really known. He was married to a great woman named Ronnie, he had three kids, and he was all about it. When we'd hang out or jabber on the job, he'd talk about his family, and I was always keen on listening since I was trying to figure out how to be a father myself. I asked him questions about kids from time to time, as I was attempting to raise my own children essentially by myself.

Though two kids were dropped off on my doorstep that fateful day I've already described to you, Kerry and Eric, I actually had three children. Kyle had a different mother, and he would split his time between his mom and me. She was also a stripper, but we were never married, and she had her struggles with dope. When we had conceived Kyle years back, I ran off to prison and then came out to find him five years old. You can imagine that it was quite a shock. Anyway, growing up, Kyle was at the whims of his mom, who I never lived with. He split his time between her home and mine about fifty-fifty, but it wasn't anything organized. When he was young, he preferred his mom's house because he could get his way with her and wear her down, so she would let him do whatever he wanted. There was discipline at my house, and he didn't like that. But when he'd get mad at his mom, or when she'd run off to jail or just run off, Kyle would come and live with me. It would be six months without him, then he would be at my place for a year, and then he'd be gone for a year, and I'd have him for three months, etc.

I thought about going after full custody for a while, but I decided not to, knowing that it would break Kyle's heart. He loved his mom, and living with her was what he knew. I figured I could either make him live with me fulltime but have him resent me, or I could sit just within reach, always ready to catch him the minute things went wrong. I got the calls from the police when his mom was getting hauled in. I was there for Kyle when he ticked somebody off and needed a place to go. My house was where he turned for refuge, eventually. I sacrificed our relationship early on so that I could do better for him, and I think that paid off in the long run.

As you can see, my family situation was complicated. Added to the mess was the fact that my stripper/wife, the woman I was currently living with, did not have much of a desire to be a mom, and consequently she was terrible at it.

You can see that I needed those long talks and all that advice from Tom.

I thought about the old life from time to time, and how it seemed like it was easier than what I had to do now, with the responsibilities and restrictions that felt new and strange.

It would get to me sometimes, and Tom and I would go down to Chicano Park some nights to blow off steam. "Some nights" may be a mischaracterization, actually. We went every day to have a beer before going home. Then every Friday after work, I'd be fed up with the frustrations of life and trying to do everything perfectly, so we'd go to Chicano Park and split a half pint of whiskey in addition to the daily 40oz.

That's a rough part of town, if you weren't aware, and it was not unknown to me that we were likely to get attacked by some junkie from time to time. That's where the blowing off steam came in, I suppose, being only too happy to decline the junkies' attempts at robbing me. They don't call me Flash for nothing.

Besides hanging out in the park after work with Tom, I'd go to a bar called Chuey's a lot with another guy from the shipyard named Fitz. We each had our designated barstools and knew every bartender by name. Ronnie wasn't much for Tom hanging out at the bar, but she wouldn't say much about him stopping for a beer at the park on the way home. Aside from confrontations with the occasional junkie, it was fairly mellow. Chuey's, on the other hand, was a lot of drinking, tough talk, and bar fights. Like I said, my road to redemption was a bumpy one, but this was part of the journey for me. Getting in scrapes with other rough dudes didn't seem like breaking the law to me then, and it certainly was a far cry from the sort of dirt I used to do.

So, for better or for worse, I was a bit of a weekend brawler, but the important thing to me was that I had a couple of solid dudes who had my back. Tom was yet another traveler going through life and trying to live right for his family. Fitz was a bit rougher around the edges, but he was loyal – a good friend at work and after. These guys helped to give me the strength to resist falling totally back into the dark side.

You can't live a good life alone.

# Chapter 16

Learning how to be the good guy is hard.

Some parts of it came naturally to me. For instance, I was a source of some stability in my son Kyle's life. At his mother's house, a lot of shady characters were constantly hanging around, but whenever my car would pull into the driveway to pick up Kyle, these dudes would scatter like cockroaches. Kyle says that he remembers to this day full-grown, tough-talking men leaping over fences to get out when I'd come around.

I still had a reputation, and I wasn't going to put up with lowlifes dragging my son into the gutter.

So, I had the "strength" part of things down. A good man is a dangerous man, and never let anyone tell you differently. But a good man is also kind when he can be, fair, wise, honest, and patient. I was better at some parts of that list than others.

I understood discipline, for one thing, and I imparted it to my children. I had four rules for them:

1) Don't wake me up. I work long and unusual hours to provide for this family, so if I'm sleeping, some-one better be bleeding for you to wake me up.

2) Absolutely no negative contact with the police. My children were to respect the law and stay out of trouble.

3) Absolutely no trouble at school. I wanted my children to get a good education, and I didn't want to lose out on income for my family because I had to drive down to some principal's office.

4) Be home at exactly 6pm for dinner every night. We eat one meal a day together, no exceptions.

As you can see, I did not have many rules, but they were gospel truth in my house. Subsequently, my kids did well in school and didn't have a criminal record. It was a different time, then, and kids were a bit safer going around town by themselves. They walked or skated to and from school, and they learned a good amount of independence, but we always, always ate dinner together, so that we could bond as a family, catch up on each other's lives, and I could share a piece or two of fatherly wisdom the best I knew how.

When my kids would commit some indiscretion, like all kids do, they were scared of me "kicking their butt." They knew my reputation as well, but for all of that sort of language they were using, I never laid a hand on my children. I remembered far too vividly what my own father had done to me as a child, and there was simply no way that I would ever do the same to my flesh and blood.

Instead, I got creative with discipline.

## Running in Circles

One time, for instance, Kyle lied to me, and you have to understand, I'm big on honesty and openness. The kids knew not to lie, and I don't remember what it was about, but my son had lied to me. So, later on, I handed him a shovel and took him to the backyard. He had a flippant attitude, I think. He liked yard work and physical labor. I had taught all of my kids not to despise hard work, and so they actually enjoyed it. As long as there was some sense of accomplishment at the end, they felt good about their sweat and time being spent. So, when I gave Kyle a shovel and a job as punishment, I'm pretty sure he was thinking, "No big deal." I told him to dig a hole three feet wide and four feet deep in a particular spot, and he got to work in a way that would make any father proud.

I assume that he thought I was going to plant a tree there or something, because he was all smiles when he finished an hour or so later and came in the house to tell me so.

"What are we going to put in there, Dad?" he asked.

"Dirt," I said.

He was confused, so I explained.

"Take all the dirt that you just dug up and put it back in the hole."

He was still confused, but he went out and did what I asked, a little bewildered. After a while, he came back inside to tell me it was done, and I told him that he needed to dig out the same hole again.

"But why? The dirt is already loose there because I dug it up. It's not going to accomplish anything!"

"Exactly," I told him. "It's sort of like lying that way, isn't it? It looks like you have an endgame in mind, and then what actually happens is you end up digging yourself in a hole, having to cover your tracks, and then tell another lie, and then you have to get out of that one too, and on and on it goes, accomplishing nothing and wearing you out in the process."

He understood it then. He's never forgotten that day, in fact. I made him dig that big old hole and fill it up again three times. He didn't lie to me after that. I don't think he lied to anyone else, either.

## Loyalty

I don't mean to pick on my son Kyle, because Eric and

Kerry needed discipline too, but this story stands out in my memory.

As I would later find out, Eric, who was about four years older than Kyle, was out with his brother on some bike jumps out on an abandoned lot somewhere. Other kids had swooped in on Eric's "turf" and took over the jumps. Eric, being something of a hothead like his father, started talking tough with these big kids and telling them off. They got angrier and angrier, until it got to the point of a physical altercation. Kyle, being four years younger, and counting that the other guys had one, two, three, four... and that he and Eric were only two, decided to just slyly step to the side and watch as his brother got into a fistfight with the numerically superior opposition. Naturally, this was a fight that Eric did not win.

Now's where I come in.

These two boys of mine trudged home after, and I saw the tell-tale signs of a scuffle all over Eric, who'd gotten beaten up pretty well, and then there was Kyle without a scratch on him. I asked what happened, and they told me.

"Why didn't you fight alongside your brother?" I asked Kyle.

"Because he was being stupid!" Kyle answered. "And there were more of those guys than us. Eric was just running his mouth, so why should I get beat up?"

"Eric," I said, "Don't go picking fights, and learn to control your tongue, but Kyle, I'm laying some discipline on you, and I want you to understand something. I don't ever want to see Eric come in beat-up again and you all squeaky clean. He's your brother, and his fights are your fights. If he ever gets beaten up again, you better have some marks on you too."

See, this may sound strange to some of you reading this, but it worked out brilliantly. On the one hand, Kyle learned to think about somebody besides just himself, and he ended up becoming very loyal to his brother, so that these two sons of mine discovered that they could lean on each other. And Eric learned that his smart mouth was going to end up causing not just himself some hurt, but it would be dragging in his innocent brother too.

They both ended up getting in less trouble after that, but whatever trouble they did get in, they got out of it together. Brothers should be a team, in my opinion.

So, there were some parts of being a dad that I had under my belt. And then... there were other parts.

OB Dave and me, getting ready for a funeral run in Oakland, CA

On a cross-country ride in Ohio.

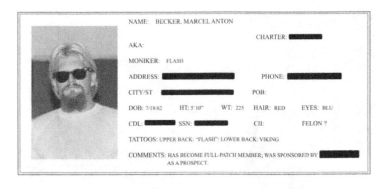

NAME: BECKER, MARCEL ANTON

CHARTER: ████████

AKA:

MONIKER: FLASH

ADDRESS: ████████  PHONE: ████████

CITY/ST ████████  POB:

DOB: 7/18/62  HT: 5'10"  WT: 225  HAIR: RED  EYES: BLU

CDL: ████████ SSN: ████████  CII:  FELON ?

TATTOOS: UPPER BACK: "FLASH"; LOWER BACK: VIKING

COMMENTS: HAS BECOME FULL-PATCH MEMBER; WAS SPONSORED BY ████████ AS A PROSPECT.

It wasn't too long until my activities earned me a dossier, courtesy of the feds. Once I was on their radar, prison became a revolving door for me.

(Left) My booking photo in El Reno Federal Penitentiary. This came after a lengthy con air flight – which was more like a multiple-stop merry-go-round. If I don't seem happy, it's because I wasn't.

(Right) My appearance changed so much during that term, they made me take another photo.

On the yard with some of the fellas. Note the high-tech penitentiary prosthesis.

Prison was a bit of a different animal in the 80s. We had official weightlifting and arm-wrestling competitions, and once we even had a Harley show that civilians came to the yard to attend. They don't have these sorts of events in prison today. The picture to the left is me with two champions from different weight classes when I won the middleweight arm-wrestling championship in El Reno.

On the yard during a different term at La Tuna F.C.I. Note the artificial background so that no prison security features such as gun towers, walls, fences, etc. can be photographed.

Prison always had its downsides, naturally. Getting stabbed, harassment from guards, getting stabbed some more... but solitary confinement was the first time a sentence really sucked all of the humor out of me. The above photo is what I looked like prior to my 18-month solitary confinement; below is after. The same guy is standing next to me in both pictures so you can compare. He didn't change. I lost eighty pounds. The clothes disguise it a little, but I was a walking skeleton.

Weightlifting competitions and bike shows don't take the dead look from your eyes after countless stabbings/attempts on your life.

Fresh out of prison and suddenly an instant dad. I had to cut ties with everyone I had known and forget many of the skills I had acquired. Still, life was better out than in.

With Kerry, my daughter, and Eric, my oldest son. These kids were my inspiration for making a clean break with crime and learning how to live as a productive, law-abiding citizen. They saved my life.

Finally working an honest job. I was out less than a year in this photo, with Kerry and Eric at take-your-kids-to-work day. It was a freeing, peaceful feeling to not have to worry about anyone finding out what I was doing: I had nothing to hide.

# Chapter 17

"Wounded people wound people."

"Once bitten, twice shy."

However you want to say it, that was me. I was freshly out of the criminal justice system, still receiving visits from my parole officer, and I had all of this weight of responsibility on my shoulders. I was a single parent before I ever got divorced, if you get my drift. Now, the problem was, no one had ever really modeled to me how to handle familial conflict well. The one point in my favor was that I was determined to never, ever hit a family member. But man, oh, man, did I have a temper. Certain things rubbed against an old hurt, and it could really be zero to sixty.

## Surprise!

I remember one time I was at home with my kids on the weekend, still at that second-story apartment on Winter Gardens, when the whole building shook violently. I ran outside and saw a big pickup truck that had just crashed through a support beam and slammed into the exterior wall of my apartment. Kyle was at his mom's, but Kerry and Eric had been playing outside. I saw Kerry, who was white as a ghost, but I didn't see Eric.

I looked down at the truck, partway smashed into the wall, and I knew that Eric was between them. He'd been playing under the stairs.

I didn't hesitate a moment. I jumped off of the second story balcony, landed on top of the truck, then leaped down to the ground, where I ran to the front of the truck, ready for the worst moment of my entire life. And then, thank God in heaven, Eric peeked around the corner, wondering what the big noise had been. He hadn't been hit after all.

The relief lasted for a moment, but it was quickly displaced by rage. I turned around on the driver of the truck, who was still in a daze in the front seat, and his equally dazed buddies in the passenger seats. The car stank of alcohol. It was just three drunk idiots who had tried to pull into a Carl's Junior drive-thru next door, but instead turned the wrong way, hopped a low wall, and plowed into my apartment building at a frightening speed.

I pulled that dude through the open window, right out of the cab, and started laying into him. His buddies were smart enough to stumble and fall out of the car, then run off. Meanwhile, I was using the driver as a punching bag and screaming at him full force about how he could have killed my son, plowing through his play area like that. I was senseless. I only had anger. I was beating the snot out of this guy, until my daughter Kerry finally succeeded in getting my attention.

I was holding this joker by the collar when I looked to see her pointing. I followed her finger, and it dawned on me what was happening, and what the consequences could be.

A crowd had gathered. People were watching. And I was definitely committing aggravated assault.

My entire vow could be ruined right then and there, because of my anger. I had a parole officer to answer to, and even if I didn't, I was still a five-time felon in a three-strikes state. One more arrest, and I would be in prison for life, relegating my children to social services.

I couldn't let that happen.

I picked the guy up, told him to beat it, and got inside as quick as I could. The guy ran off, of course, not wanting to stick around for a DD and whatever else was coming to him. Inside my apartment, I waited around, expecting the worst but hoping for one last streak of luck. I'd been pretty fortunate in the past with dodging bullets, both literal and figurative, and I really needed this to blow over.

Thankfully, no one called the cops on me, or if they did, nothing came of it. My vow was intact. I was still guardian of these kids.

Now, of course any father would be angered by the recklessness of that driver, but for all of my years in martial arts and as a loyal biker, I suddenly realized that I had no control. Once the anger hit me, I was running down that path with nothing to stop me.

But that's not when I really knew that it was a problem. My behavior here was too easy to explain away.

## "You're Crazy!"

I don't know if I've mentioned this before or not, but my stripper/wife was not a paragon of reasonableness and virtue. She was not a good stepmother. She was barely even coherent when times got tough, and yet my demons were quick to raise their head as well.

Naturally we fought a lot. She loved the old me – the important, influential criminal in a tough biker gang who scored a lot of great dope and brought home plenty of money for other shady activities. Now I was a blue-collar worker who did long hours and wanted to teach his children about honesty and discipline.

Disagreements arose.

But, as there always is, there was one particular fight. It wasn't going well. We were arguing and screaming like usual, but my stripper/wife turned her back on me, said she was done, and slammed a door in my face. Well, she may have been done, but I was not, and I still had a good piece that I wanted to say. As a lifelong martial artist, a little door between us was nothing. I had a psychotic karate instructor who made me break boards until I bled and bruised. One little side kick and that door was flat on the ground.

I, naturally, continued on my earlier discourse. The only thing was, the kids were there. So there I am, a big, scary man kicking down doors and yelling, and I see my stripper/wife cradling my son's head away from me. She yelled, "You're crazy!" and ran past me. In a few moments, she'd gotten Kerry as well, and you better believe I heard a car engine shortly after. All of a sudden I was alone, left to consider my actions, my anger, and the look in my family's eyes when they saw me.

It was terror.

Do you know what it's like to have a loved one look at you with *dread*? My own children were scared of me, and not in a "healthy respect" sort of a way. They were terrified, and I was left with the inescapable conclusion that I had a real problem.

After sitting on the steps with my head in my hands for a healthy length of time, I got up and did what any self-respecting ex-con would do. I called my lawyer.

I needed advice. I told him that I never hit my kids or my woman, but it was becoming clear to me that my anger was not under my control. It was a problem, and I didn't know what to do about it. He recommended a certain guy who was an expert in criminal profiling and psychology who ran a specialized anger management course.

In the past, I would have laughed at the idea, but at rock bottom, you realize how weak you really are, your flaws loom large, and you realize that something needs to change.

The one-on-one sessions lasted three years, and they were extraordinarily expensive, but on that day I made one more call asking for advice from my brother Mike, and he went around and arranged to pay for the anger management. I never would have been able to pay for it on my own.

I might just owe my brother my life, or at least owe him the fact that I was able to stay out of prison for the rest of my life.

I learned a lot about myself during those anger management sessions. I learned about the old wounds from my dad, from childhood, from bullies, enemies, and loneliness. In therapy, we worked those wounds over until I no longer had an automatic, explosive reaction to those old triggers.

It took years, but I became a patient man – which helped with the parenting quite a bit. But even more than that, the experience humbled me again. It reminded me that we all need to seek help sometimes, and only a fool tries to keep stumbling on by himself in those seasons.

So, home life was a struggle, and so was work. Difficulty defined my existence.

But I didn't give up. I swallowed my pride, put my head down, and did what needed to be done. My kids still had me, and no matter what came against me, I was going to conquer the docks, too.

# Chapter 18

I hustled, worked above and beyond the call of duty, and refused to be ashamed of the tasks that were given to me at my station of "Assistant Boot-licker." When I scrubbed toilets, I did so with pride. When I was back in the SHU program in prison, I lived with a toilet only inches from where I slept, so I was quite proficient in making them shine. It didn't matter that cleaning toilets, running errands, or sweeping up "wasn't my job." I was there on the docks to go legit, and as far as I saw it, every other guy working around me was the competition. I showed up a few minutes early every day, took a shorter lunch than everyone else, and left a little later than the others.

Finally, this sort of thing got me noticed.

I made full "Boot-licker."

Alright, those weren't our real titles, but you get the idea. My little promotion and raise had a significant effect on my life at this point, however. I went from $5.50 an hour to making ten bucks, and with overtime, I could live on ten bucks an hour back then. I quit my job bouncing at the strip club, knowing that it was only a matter of time until I got into some old trouble back there. I was fully legit now.

Aside from the occasional bar fight.

## Friendly Terms

This was the first taste of freedom I'd ever really had in my life. Let me tell you something; freedom isn't just roaming around doing whatever you want to. I'd tried that, and it had more than its fair share of complications. Freedom is being where you're meant to be, doing what you ought to be doing, and being content. Sure, my stripper/wife was a terrible mother and, increasingly, a terrible wife. Sure, we were barely living above the poverty line. And yes, I hadn't exactly figured out how to be Ward Cleaver as a father yet, but I was trying. And when you're trying to do the right thing, that's a breath of fresh air because you don't have anything to hide.

Whenever my parole officer would come by in the old days, I would say as little as humanly possible. I would only let him in my place if he showed me a warrant. I'd be standoffish, and I certainly wouldn't volunteer any information or show any sort of kindness to the guy. Cops are the enemy, right?

Well, now here I was with a clean conscience. When my PO would show up, I had a big smile on my face. I'd invite him and his partner inside. I'd say, "Hey! How are you doing? You want a can of soda? Have a seat. What do you want to know?" I was doing well. I had decided to go straight for my kids, and dang it, I was succeeding.

That's the funny thing about this vow as opposed to the last one: there's always another guy trying to intimidate you, always another monster that you've got to outdo to prove your toughness. But with trying to live on the right side of the law and put food on the table, it was measureable. I felt like I was accomplishing something, even when our circumstances weren't all that glamorous. There weren't any negative side-effects of doing the right thing, other than dealing with the occasional critic and a financial squeeze.

So, I hate to be a pessimist, but it can't come as too much of a surprise to you that another crisis was about to rear its head.

## "You're Fired!"

The two words every parolee dreads are, "you're fired," particularly in my case. Idle hands are the devil's workshop, as they say, and it turns out a parole board doesn't look kindly on the devil's handiwork. One of the stipulations of my release from prison was that I remain gainfully employed, and after a few months of feeling like things were just starting to work out, the shipyard economy suddenly slowed down, and the layoffs started.

Don't accuse me of being overdramatic, but it was like a horror movie. Every day, you didn't know who just wasn't going to be there, because his job got erased. You didn't know if it would be you, your buddy, or one of the critics, but what we all knew was that plenty of people were getting the ax. And who was especially vulnerable?

New guys.

I was a new guy. I was a new guy who had just gotten a raise, and that was a problem for the budget. As more and more guys got fired, it wasn't paranoia telling me I was next. It was the simple truth. I was going to lose my job.

I couldn't let that happen.

I was still fresh out from prison, all things considered. I still had that scarlet letter hung around my neck. I couldn't just walk to the nearest haberdashery and offer my services – it was the docks or nothing for me at that point. So, I did a search of open positions at my company, and I found that they were looking for a "Facilities Department Planner."

I didn't have the faintest clue what a department planner did, but what I did know was that it was a job no one wanted. Every new guy washed out a couple of months into the job, and people were avoiding it like the plague. So, I went ahead and applied, figuring, "Heck, it'll take them at least three months to figure out I'm a fraud. Then, if I get fired, at least that's three more months of work than I would have had otherwise." I didn't care if the work was pleasant or not. I was just trying to survive.

Lo and behold, they gave me the job. My first task: Figuring out what in the heck I was supposed to be doing.

# Chapter 19

It's a funny thing, having a job and having no idea what that job actually entails. I don't know that I expected to succeed, but I certainly wasn't going to sit around feeling sorry for myself. I had kids now, and I'd made a vow to make it on the up and up for their sake.

The first thing I did was make discrete inquiries about what a facilities planner actually did. Turns out, they were responsible for coordinating the docking of ships that needed repair, as well as providing whatever support systems were needed. So I needed to make sure we had transportation for sailors disembarking the craft, that we were hooking up water, power, compressed air, and other vital services (on a huge navy ship, this is a bit more difficult than just plugging in a cord). I had to make sure the rounds were happening on all the ships, keeping the temporary services maintained and monitored. Perhaps, most critically, I had to keep dozens and dozens of people on time so that projects got done.

Now this probably doesn't sound all that bad to the uninitiated. "Why did so many people quit this position?" you might be asking.

Timing is a delicate thing, and people want what they want when they want it. If a group of sailors has to wait around an hour for transportation, somebody's going to hear about it. If there's no electricity yet, the craftsmen can't start their work on time, and somebody's going to hear about it. If water's not getting pumped up to the ship as soon as it's docked, somebody is sure to complain. And guess where the buck stops and the blame begins? With the guy in charge of support services.

Facilities planners get yelled at a lot.

And it's a strange thing – people don't like to be yelled at. They don't like the buck to stop with them. There are a million variables outside of your control when coordinating mammoth tasks on such large ships, and so people tend to wash out after about six months. It's easy to get discouraged when you're trying your best but things go wrong and you get criticism.

To make matters worse, this is a business where relationships are very important for actually getting work done, and I was the new guy. My calls got dodged a lot. The odds were stacked against me on every project, and I was one big failure away from getting the boot – which I formerly licked. And getting fired meant trouble with the parole board.

I could have easily washed out in six months like all those other guys, but I had two secret weapons.

The first was a positive attitude, and maybe not quite in the way you'd expect.

Yes, of course I was grateful for the work, I was used to criticism, and I didn't take pity on myself. Those things are essential. But this is what I did when I ran up against a wall and I couldn't get something scheduled, or things were taking too much time, too much money, or somebody told me a situation was impossible: I just drew on my previous experience, from my time on the dark side of life.

Those of you who have a history of addiction will relate to this. Before I went straight, I was a regular, recreational drug user. So, when Friday night would roll around, I'd call up my guy and tell him I needed some supplies for a good time. Except sometimes, this dealer of mine would be laying low, unavailable, or out of my drug of choice. Do you think I just hung up the phone, said, "Oh well," and went to bed early? Surely not! I pulled out my little black book and called everybody I knew – and if I needed to, I had them call everybody *they* knew. I had an addiction to feed, and no matter how scarce my drug was or how hard to get, you can bet that by 10:00 p.m. I had what I was after, and enough of it to keep me high through Sunday.

That, of course, is a stupid way to use determination and perseverance. But what it taught me was that there's no sense in throwing your hands up. If I could get it done for something so trivial and selfish as a fix on the weekends, I could find a way to get a hold of that journeyman who's ignored twenty-five of my calls. I was relentless, no matter what the obstacle was. If we were out of supplies and nobody had the hoses, wires, or whatever that we needed, I found it or I found somebody who could find it.

As it turned out, I was pretty good at being a facilities planner. When I had first applied to the job, I didn't write "Inmate Tank Captain," "Money Launderer," or "Former Drug Addict" on my resume, but bizarrely, those experiences had something to teach me.

This is part of a broader life principle, I think. Attitude is everything. Yes, I imagine my life would have been better if I'd never needed to become a tank captain in prison, played around with illegal money, or if I had never started doing drugs in the old days, but there is something to be learned from every experience. Failures and foolish paths have a lot to teach us if we have the right perspective about them. That's no reason to choose failure and foolishness, but looking back on it from the other side can be a help.

So that was one of my secret weapons against the odds. The other wasn't something I could have come up with myself. Secret weapon number two was a man named Jim Clark.

# Chapter 20

Jim Clark was the sort of man who was going to do things his way, regardless of criticism. He was smart, a college graduate with twenty years in the navy. He was African American, and being older than me as he was, his marriage to a white woman named Dianne came during a time where that sort of thing was viewed quite unfavorably. I know that didn't ruffle Jim's feathers one bit.

He had an enormous amount of will and moral character. He set the bar high and led from the front, always keeping you accountable to his clearly-defined expectations. He was ballsy, innovative, and exceptionally successful.

I respected the hell out of him.

Now, even though I was bound and determined to make this new life work, I still had my doubts and my fears from time to time. There were some nights, sitting up awake, staring at the floor, where I thought it was all going to come crashing down around me at any moment. It was easy to fall into despair about the old scarlet letter around my neck that said, "Ex-con." So, it was of critical importance to me both personally and professionally that a guy named Jim Clark passed through my life.

When I took on the facilities planner job, Jim was my boss. He was a perceptive guy, and he made it very clear to me early on that he cared about the work we were doing, not the pasts of the people doing it. He said to me once, "I'm just going to measure you by what you do today."

This was life-changing for me. Goodbye scarlet letter. Here was a place where I could rise or fall on the sweat of my brow and the strength of my mind. I was given more and more responsibility as I proved myself, and I was treated the same as all of the other guys we worked around.

It felt good. It felt free.

I'll never forget an early performance review that he gave me. Jim wrote, "Marcel is hardworking, capable, and has an uncanny grasp of issues well beyond his formal education." Hearing this from someone as intelligent and educated as Jim struck a chord in me. It gave me confidence. It kicked the tail of those ghosts telling me I was just an imposter in this world. I had a job, I was good at it, and my boss told me that I belonged.

If there was one person who made a difference in my life when I needed it the most, it was Jim Clark.

## On the Up and Up

Now, success certainly involves determination, a positive attitude, and skill, but I'd be lying to you if I said that fortunate timing didn't have a role to play. You can call it luck, but personally, I'll call it providence that I ended up working under Jim, because his star was on the rise. As he got promoted and placed on bigger and more prestigious projects, he took me with him. And my star rose too.

To understand the scope of the projects we undertook at this company, you have to know what sort of work we were doing. We would take large ships, mostly naval ships, up on a dry dock and out of the water. That alone is a feat. Then, we run power, water, sanitation, and in the old days steam to the ship so that it can continue to function as we work on it. Then, we renovate and fix it up – the entire thing. Imagine all of the work that goes into renovating a high-rise apartment building in New York City. That's sort of what this was like, except a ranking official in the U.S. Military is going to be there at the end of it to inspect your work.

Some people have called it stressful. Personally, I loved

the challenge.

Early on in my tenure as facilities planner in the production support services craft, the shipyard had what can only be described as an epic shipbuilding project. My company got the contract to renovate a mini aircraft carrier, and believe me, there was nothing "mini" about it. 840 compartments (galleys, dining halls, sleeping quarters, etc.) had to be signed of and closed. Sounds great, right? The only hitch was that we had just thirty days to do it, and the navy was watching.

But now I'm getting ahead of myself. First, I have to tell you about getting tossed to the wolves and making it out alive.

So there I was in facilities, making a career out of this job that formerly had been a leap of desperation. Then, as waterfront companies are wont to do, we got bought out by another mid-level private equity firm that came in to clean house. The guy this new company assigned to my department did not rub me the right way. There's quite a bit more to it than that, of course, but the long and the short of it is that this guy had me in his sights for termination once the purchase and transition of our company was complete. Jim Clark saw that. He knew it. And, looking out for me like he was, he sent me to the only job that no one was dumb enough to take:

Superintendent of this epic shipbuilding project I've just described to you.

They were shorthanded and needed someone to take the reins on closing these compartments. What does closing a compartment look like? It means we had to make sure that every single habitable quarter was up to code on construction, carpentry, painting, electrical, plumbing... I could go on and make this a really long list, but I'll spare you. Everything in these rooms had to be pristine, and that required a lot of coordinating different craftsmen. When a room (or compartment) was entirely finished, up to code, inspected, and approved, we said it was "closed."

Now why would this be such a challenge? Look at it this way; refurbishing and repairing ships is a lot like building or remodeling a house. In other words, it's a logistical nightmare. Add in the fact that there are strict deadlines and you are working for the fighting forces of the United States government, and that only adds to the need for things to get done right and on time – but that means excellent coordination. Here's how it often goes:

Making sure that the framer is done with his work on time is crucial, because the drywall guy can't start until he is. And the painter can't start until the drywall is totally finished. On any given job, we might have plumbing, electrical, engineeering, carpentry, flooring, inspections, client visits, sanitation, maintenance, and technical workers thrown into the mix as well. If just one tiny thing is out of place, this entire train that we've established derails, rolls down a mountainside, and explodes.

And we had 840 different rooms to do this way in only thirty days.

In retrospect, I think that no one expected this project to succeed. The timeline was simply impossible given the sheer volume of work and coordination required. So, what my company needed was a fall guy, someone who was new enough that a gigantic failure could be blamed on his inexperience while saving face for the navy. They could call it bungling by an employee that, don't worry, surely won't be working here for long. And that way they get to tell the navy, "No, no, it wasn't an unreasonable request, this new guy just messed things up." The only question was, who would be the fall guy?

I'll describe him to you: He has two thumbs, and it's me.

# Chapter 21

So there I was, all set up to fail on this epic shipbuilding project, but no one had the courtesy to tell me so. Thankfully, my ignorance and inexperience proved to be a help at this time because I didn't know what couldn't be done. 840 compartments sounded like a lot, but that was what was asked of me. All I knew was that I had a family to feed, a boss that believed in me, and a heck of a job to do.

So, I got to work.

Business as usual wasn't going to cut it this time. I knew that much. We had to close an average of nearly thirty compartments a day for thirty days in a row, and I'd heard too many stories of chasing down subcontractors, apprentices dodging calls, and trying to get two trades to communicate with each other. I had no intention of trying to herd cats. I needed a new approach that provided accountability and centralized this scattered mess of a to-do list on each compartment.

The solution? A tiger team.

For those of you raising your eyebrows, Siegfried and Roy, Joe Exotic, and Tony the Tiger had nothing to do with this. A tiger team is essentially a group consisting of one representative from each trade that will be needed in closing up a compartment. I had an electrician, pipe fitter, lagger, painter, etc., all part of the same unit, and I forced them to work together, not separately. When we did our preliminary inspections of each room, I made every single member of each tiger team go and look it over together. They coordinated amongst themselves, saw where more work was needed from each trade in particular rooms, communicated, and avoided the bottlenecks so common in this kind of work. The work we identified on the daily inspections was turned over to the night shifts for completion, and on the next inspection the compartments were closed.

On the docks, this was completely novel. It just wasn't how we did things. But the stakes were high, and I was willing to take a risk. Long story short, it paid off in a big way. We closed every single one of those 840 compartments in under a month, and the top brass at the company was astounded. My tiger team approach slowly began to spread throughout the industry after this project, and to this day it's been one of the two innovations I have come up with that have changed how my industry does work.

So, I was the fall guy who was too dumb to fall, and my boss was too decent to hog the credit. His star rose, and mine rose with it.

## Consequences

For much of my life up till this point, "consequences" had been an unpleasant word, but the truth of the matter is that you get out what you put in. When I was on the dark side of life, I was experiencing a lot of negative consequences due to the illegality and barbarity of my actions. Now that I had vowed to go straight for my kids' sakes, "consequences" was no longer a swear word. I began to see rewards for how I was living and working. It was a breath of fresh air and a long time coming.

Before I get into the specifics, you have to understand that all of this is coming from a guy whose dad couldn't keep a job. He had his own hardships, and that doesn't excuse the reality of it or make it any worse either, but the fact is that he never achieved greatness or even stability in work. Having a successful career was a huge deal for me. I never saw myself that way growing up. My brother Mike, he was the successful one, and I thought I was destined to be the loser. But now, finally, I felt respectable. I had a few wins on my record. Competence breeds confidence, as they say, and I began to hold my head high.

Succeeding on the epic shipbuilding project launched me to new heights in my career. I'd been on the docks about four years at that point, and I got promoted again and given more responsibility. Most importantly, I got noticed.

The group of people that noticed me called themselves "The A-Team," and no one disputed their right to the title. They were the only group on the West Coast to have won the Aegis Flag for excellence in their work, the best of the best. My tiger team approach intrigued them, and I was assigned to start working with them.

It was truly an honor. Working with individuals who are better than you in some capacity – more experienced, sharper, better educated, etc. – makes you better. Iron sharpens iron, and I was quite pleased to be invited into their ranks.

I learned more about business inside the A-Team than at any other point in my life, largely due to two great men who would go on to become mentors to me on this next stage of my journey: Bob Koerber and Marty Fischer.

# Chapter 22

They were both tall. That's about where the similarities between Bob and Marty ended.

Bob had a storied career coming into the waterfront, and he when he had been brought in, he started near the top. Marty, on the other hand, had worked his way up from the bottom. He started as a carpenter and became an executive, with a few intermediate steps, as you might imagine. Bob pulled you along with him. Marty pushed you from behind. Bob's default setting was to see the work through the eyes of our clients. Marty's default setting was to see it through the eyes of our subcontractors. Bob saw the end, and Marty saw the process.

They were polar opposites in just about every way, and they were also the single most effective leadership duo I've ever come across in my life.

Let's start with Marty.

He was 6'1" or 6'2", wore a full beard all of the time and had glasses. He was predominantly bald and ethnically Swiss. Marty was a smart guy, self-made, and I think he had the words "schedule compliance" tattooed on the inside of his eyelids.

Marty was never late. No one who worked for Marty was ever late. If there was a problem in that respect, he fixed it real quick. Everything was about earned value, a concept that I learned from him. Time is money, and wasting money's how you go out of business. So everything, down to the last detail, would be analyzed, evaluated, and scheduled. The resulting schedule was not so much a living, breathing document as it was the law etched in stone.

Marty pushed you. He pushed you to be better. He

wanted to squeeze out every ounce of value and potential that you had in you. No excuses were allowable, because you can be better, and such progress was always expected.

Maybe this all sounds rigid, but he was productive as heck. He was a man who accomplished things and let others in on his secrets, so they could accomplish things too. He was team-oriented, driven, and intense.

Then there was Bob.

He was a little bit shorter than Marty but not much. Stoic. Kind. He was a man of deep faith and conviction, but there was something else about him too.

You see, when you come from the sort of world that I grew up in, you gain a sixth sense for sizing people up. You know who's a threat and who isn't. You know who has nerve and who doesn't. Everyone has this ability to some extent, but when your life regularly depends on it (cops, criminals, soldiers, etc.), this ability gets honed to a level of reliability not much different than sight.

Bob Koerber was a soft-spoken, kind man, but I knew that he was lethal. You could see the steel in his eyes if you knew what to look for. He was dangerous, but he was good. Seeing that to such a degree in another person gave me something to aspire to.

I called him "The Quiet Giant."

He was a graduate of the Naval Academy and had spent years in the service and the reserve building up an extremely impressive military career. He had been a member of the special warfare community in the navy and commanded one of the special boat units that sail into harm's way to deliver S.E.A.L. teams and stuff like that. He had a risky job, and he thrived in it. After his years of full-time service, he remained active in the reserve for a long time, making full 06-captain as a reservist, which is not easy to do. At one point he was even tapped as a candidate for admiral, and he would have made it too, but there was a war on in the Middle East, and they took those billets away from navy reservists. When Bob had come to work on the docks, he came in with a choir of angels singing behind him, but his head was none the bigger for it.

He had very little ego, which was odd to me at first, but refreshing. He wasn't insecure or falsely modest; he just wasn't overly concerned with himself. In his mind, his concerns were God, people, and the job, in that order, and he excelled at everything he put his hands to. Bob is the person who taught me about "servant leadership," only he didn't call it that. He just lived it. He led from the front.

Bob had more leadership in his little finger than most boardrooms have in the totality of persons present. Between him and Marty, I was taught how to work at a higher level, how to lead people successfully, and how to win. They ran a meritocracy, like Jim Clark had, where a man can rise or fall on his performance and ingenuity.

I spent four years working under these gentlemen, and the value of that time is unquantifiable.

Eventually, a private equity firm became interested in buying out the company, and Marty took his life's savings – about $100,000 – and invested in the company. When the company was sold, he walked away with millions, retiring at age fifty. Bob stuck around longer. He worked his way up the rest of what there still was to climb, eventually becoming vice president and general manager of the whole shipyard.

I had two great mentors, and I learned how to be an excellent worker, manager, and provider. Work was going well.

I didn't have much in the way of mentors for my home life. That was a confusing mess that, even as I was succeeding at my job, began to unravel in my hands.

# Chapter 23

My career was going well, and my family was in shambles.

I felt like I'd won the "parent of the year" award, not due to my own quality but rather the deficiencies of the competition.

It was like I had won a long-drive contest by using a putter, but there was only one other contestant, and they were swinging at the golf ball with a stalk of celery. I may not have had the best tool for the job, but at least it was still a golf club. The ball still wasn't getting very far down the green.

I'll pull back from the metaphors and tell you straight. I was not equipped to be the greatest father, and I knew that, but my stripper/wife was a horrible, horrible mother.

In her (slight) defense, being a mom in a mixed family is a difficult thing – especially when your husband's an ex-biker, there's alcohol in the mix, none of the kids are yours biologically, and you make your living from doing things we don't discuss in polite society.

We weren't living in polite society.

I did have some trouble understanding my children, and I raised my voice a few times when I shouldn't have, but I also tried to model good character for them. I provided a living, put food on the table, and taught them what I knew how to teach. My stripper/wife on the other hand, she never really wanted to be a mother. Conflict turned into physical assault pretty quickly, and seeing a kid get hit never sat right with me. Some things can get smoothed over when you're trying to hold a family together, but I was beginning to suspect that I needed to get my kids away from this lady.

I wasn't dad of the year, but at least I wasn't the devil.

## Blast from the Past

These things weighed on me. I would throw myself into my work and do well there, but I also knew that the whole point of me doing this in the first place was for those kids of mine. Something had to give, and it had to be soon.

So let me rewind the clock a little bit here. At this point, I hadn't been promoted to the A-Team yet. I was still working under Jim Clark, working closely with my former foreman Tom Wright, and I had a long way to go but still enough influence and authority to hire and fire people, as well as to affect our work in a substantive way.

And it was at this point (family in shambles, doing ok at work) that my phone rang, and I heard a familiar voice on the other side asking for a job.

It was Ron.

My old biker friend, my confidant, my (alleged) partner in crime. I hadn't spoken to him in a few years because when I decided to live within the boundaries of the law, he was still pushing the limits. But that day, he asked me for a job. He said that he needed to get out of the old life, and he needed a place to start.

I was uniquely positioned to be sympathetic to that pitch.

Loyalty means a lot to me, and I was of course ready to do anything to bring my old friend on at the company, but I told him he was going to have to study for the pee test.

For those of you who are blissfully unaware of the vagaries and lingo of the dark side of the law, I was telling him, "You have to take a drug test, stupid. If you're still doing the drugs that I know you used to love so well, kiss that job goodbye, and you'll be making me look bad, too."

He said, "No, no, I'm good, man. No studying needed. I'm clean."

So we brought him in, and he was as good as his word. And I got to see a little bit of my former life restored to me, but transformed and made right.

Ron meant it when he said that he was done doing his old dirt. He wanted to do honest work, and he threw himself into it admirably. I got my old friend back and subsequently had someone to talk to who understood my struggles and doubts better than anyone else I knew.

It was a good thing.

Ron, the old spook from Vietnam, the short-statured killer and criminal, was working alongside me on the waterfront. There was no drugs or theft or murder going on. No conspiracies, rackets, or death threats. It was just work, and you could look at yourself in the mirror at the end of the day without feeling disgusted. It was freeing. It was life.

## Changes

So, a friend showed up when I needed one, as my stripper/wife and I began going through a divorce. I took the kids. She took her "freedom." I think I got the better end of the deal.

I moved us out to Ron's place at first, and then to some apartments in El Cajon. Shortly after, Cal Trans pulled imminent domain on Ron because they were putting in a freeway coincidentally where his house was. So, Ron and I came to an agreement where I would buy a duplex if he'd agree to rent the second house from me, which gave me the income I needed to qualify for the place anyhow.

Now, instead of being raised by a stripper and an ex-biker, my kids were being raised by an ex-biker dad and his ex-biker buddy. Surprisingly, this was in fact a monumental improvement.

Unsurprisingly, it was a pretty strange house sometimes, but we made it work.

# Chapter 24

The divorce happened, but it wasn't my first rodeo. The kids did well in the new place, and as it turns out, Ron was probably better at being a father than me. He had his own unit and everything, but he'd come over for meals and stuff. Since we were neighbors and close friends anyhow, he pitched in and helped with some of the parenting too. After all, the epic shipbuilding project happened, I got promoted, and juggling a fast-track career to the executive level with three kids ain't easy.

Ron was more patient than I was. The kids liked him a lot. He was like an uncle to them, and he helped me out quite a bit.

Jim Clark continued to be a good friend. He'd invite the kids and me up to the cabin he and Dianne called home up on Palomar Mountain, and we would attend the volunteer firehouse chili cook-offs, the pit beef barbecues, and everything that goes on up there in the summers.

Tom Wright kept around, too, but unfortunately not quite in the way any of us would have preferred.

## Hard Times

Previously in this recounting, I referred to Tom as "high mileage and hard-living." Turns out, that sort of thing catches up with you at some point. He was still a family man teaching me about how to be a dad, he was still strong of mind and will – stubborn about the sorts of things you should be stubborn about – but he was no longer sound of body.

Tom was sick. And it seemed like he kept getting sicker. It was a heart condition, and it weakened him quite a bit. I had since surpassed him in terms of the company hierarchy, so I wanted to do what I could to keep him around and take care of him, and thankfully, Jim Clark was of the same opinion. Tom couldn't just stop working. He had a family to feed, and besides, he was too proud to have gone that route. Dock work is no walk in the park, though, so we came to an agreement where I would take over Tom's responsibilities and he would move to a more administrative position. We gave him a nice desk job and always made sure he had plenty of paperwork to keep him off of his feet.

I still talked with Tom. He was my friend. But as I rose on the company ladder, my daily routine no longer intersected with his quite so often.

So, it was devastating when I got the call from Ron.

"Flash," Ron yelled at me over the line. "It's Tom. You've got to get up here to the Talon Building."

That was more than enough to get my sorry butt out of the shipyard on the double.

When I got there, I saw Tom on the ground. Big, strong, rough-and-tumble Tom, sprawled out on his back where he had collapsed, wheezing with every breath. They had called the paramedics, of course, who were already on their way. We tried CPR. And when nothing else worked, I held his head in my arms.

Tom Wright wasn't the first person to have died in my arms. Unfortunately, he wasn't the last either. But he was the first friend I'd lost since starting this new life, and I had a respect and admiration for him that I've felt for few others. He was my first real friend on the docks. He helped keep me sane when it seemed like I couldn't handle the civilian life. He mentored me, drove me to work for years, gave me a fair shot in my job, and as I held him, I knew that he was gone.

I knew that he was gone the moment I'd walked into the room, to be honest. When you've seen a lot of death, you learn to feel it. You sense it. You know when someone's soul has left the building and they aren't coming back.

The medics came, strapped him up, and tied a whole network of tubes all over his body. They managed to keep him alive (at least, their definition of "alive," which basically means breathing on a machine) for a very short time, giving his wife Ronnie the chance to come and say goodbye in the hospital.

And that was it. Tom was gone.

I didn't know the rhyme or reason of it. It was sudden, but not. Unexpected, but not really. Just because you know something's coming doesn't always soften the blow.

We cried for him, and more than a few stiff drinks were raised in his honor.

Losing brothers at arms was part of the deal when I was in organized crime. It wasn't supposed to be this way out on the light side of life. I wasn't naïve, and I was certainly not unfamiliar with loss. Death's as sure a thing as anything in this world, but this one hit me hard. Tom was not just like a big brother to me, he was practically a life coach. Every day as we'd drive to work, he'd talk me through my problems, teaching me, challenging me. When he died, it was like I lost a part of myself. His passing made me stop and consider who Marcel "Flash" Becker really was. I had a career that was going well, and I knew that my purpose was to take care of my children, but beyond that, I knew more about who I wasn't than who I was.

I wasn't the bad guy anymore, and I knew who I was doing all this for. I just no longer had a clear identity.

Some losses hit you that way.

# Chapter 25

It's always something.

If you don't have any money, then you'll have problems associated with that. If you do have money, maybe you'll figure out that you have personal problems. If you don't have personal problems, maybe you've got health problems.

The way it seems to me, life always has a trick or two up her sleeve, and I don't say this as a pessimist but as someone who is trying to be pragmatic. There's always another bridge to cross.

Home life settled down for me somewhat after the divorce and the series of moves. So, it shouldn't have been any surprise that work would suddenly go sideways.

## The Glass Ceiling

I was on the fast track. I had started at the bottom as assistant boot-licker, and over the course of just a handful of years, I was in a place of prominence and responsibility, headed for an executive role. But then, once again, a private equity firm showed up and bought out our company.

I was in a good spot, with plenty of gold stars next to my name, so I wasn't worried about losing my job or anything. Sure, this new management had a different way of doing things, but I could be flexible. I was up for a promotion, and when the time came... they hired from the outside.

It was disappointing. I had been working towards a senior management role for some time, and I was the obvious choice. But I remembered how important a positive attitude is, so I put my head down and kept working, chalking it up to some bad luck or oversight.

About six months later, the same sort of position opened up again, and once more I was the person who had been groomed to fill the role.

And once again, the company hired from the outside. In both cases, a retiring military official who was looking for civilian work was awarded the job. I don't want to say that it was a "sweet deal" kind of a set-up, but it was undeniable that I was no longer living in the meritocracy that had allowed me to rise so quickly through the ranks. All of a sudden, it did matter that I had a criminal record but didn't have a college degree. The quality of my work was now less important than my "about me" section.

As time went on, it became clear that these were not idle fears. The new management viewed those who had been with the company for a long time as second-class citizens, and any leadership needed to be brought in from the outside. I was stuck. I had hit what they call the "glass ceiling," and I wasn't going anywhere.

It was a point of crisis for me. I had been happy with the progress in my career, but I had to grapple with the question of whether or not I could be content in my current role for another twenty-five or thirty years. It wasn't a bad job, but to never advance, never gain a stake in the company?

I couldn't do it. I wasn't ready to stop. I had ambition, drive, and I wanted to model something for my kids about overcoming. It was time to make a move.

## Out of the Frying Pan, into the Fire

I sat and thought hard. I needed to jump ship and tie onto a company where I could move up into senior management. It wasn't long until I thought of the perfect solution: A little company that we'll just call "Docks Inc."

Docks Inc. was a subcontractor that I had been working with for about two years, and they naturally did quite a lot of project management. The downside of working with them was that they were absolutely terrible at project management. It was embarrassing. They couldn't have managed their way out of a public restroom with two hands and a treasure map, but they had a large network. So, whenever I needed a labor pool, I called them up for one, and I did the managing myself.

We had a friendly working relationship, and I knew that they respected me, so I decided to give them a call and swing for the fences. "I'm looking to come work for you," I told them, "but this is what I want: A role in senior management and equity in the company itself. I'll earn it; you've seen the quality of my work. I'll increase your business and make it run more efficiently and profitably, and when I hit the agreed-upon benchmarks for revenue and profitability, you give me an equity position."

It was a good pitch, I thought, and I had the reputation to back it up. After several interviews they said, "Yes," but then they added a condition I hadn't anticipated.

The company was bankrupt. I had 90 days to make them financially soluble – get them to a place where they were bringing money in and had reached an agreement with their lenders for repayment – or else Docks Inc. would cease to exist.

That complicated things a bit. My choice was this: Stay at the company where I was, where there was no hope for advancement, or move to Docks Inc. and risk having the company disappear in less than three months, meaning I'd be starting from square one, this time without a job in my back pocket.

It wasn't even a question for me. I jumped onto that sinking ship and got to work.

I like a challenge, and even though it was chancy, I had my past experiences to draw on. At this point, I was risking being out of work. In the past, when a crisis would come that demanded action, the risks were more along the lines of "go to jail forever" and "you and those you love die." This career risk didn't seem so bad to me. Success meant a better life for my kids, so I was going to succeed. It really was as simple as that.

## Turning the Ship Around

I was not coming into the situation blind. To my benefit, I was already intimately familiar with Docks Inc. and I was well aware of where they were bleeding financially. I knew where they were inefficient, who could be relied upon and who couldn't, and I came in swinging with both fists – metaphorically. By this point, my days of inviting people into the boiler room for a chat were pretty much over. I found other, better ways of handling conflict, but I was still firm, resolute, and hell-bent on getting it done.

The biggest issue that they had was run-away overtime costs. In an industry where overtime is the norm, it must be judiciously managed, and Docks Inc. had absolutely no control. To make matters worse, they worked a 4/10 (four days a week, ten hours a day) in an industry that works five days a week, which for all intents and purposes created a third overtime day. Instead of time and a half restricted to Saturday and Sunday, they had Friday as an overtime day as well.

The first move I made was to return everyone to a five-day work week, eliminating that extra overtime day. The next move I made was to restructure the old overtime incentives. Many of the foremen at this company had an incentive to work overtime because they were paid hourly.

They weren't bad guys, but it's human nature – do we hustle and get the work done before work hours end, or does it look like we'll need to keep working at 150 percent of our typical wage? Unsurprisingly, many of these foremen regularly pushed work into overtime hours. To stop this, I promoted them to salaried manager positions and gave them hefty raises. Since they were salaried, there was no longer a desire to work the weekends with their crews, and overtime was dramatically reduced, which freed up cash to service the debt.

Ninety days later, the company was no longer bankrupt, the revenue had grown precipitously, and we had agreements with all of our lenders, leaving me in a senior management role with 5 percent ownership of the company.

Not bad for a five-time loser, former addict, ex-biker, social misfit.

My life had changed for the better, and I was hungry for more.

See, this is a problem that I see in a lot of people: When the crisis is past, they stop hustling. They take a vacation. As far as I was concerned, I had an opening, and I had to take it while it was still there. I wasn't satisfied with saving the company and then leaving it how it was. I was part owner now, and I had a stake in the health of Docks Inc. I put my head down and got to work.

Part of my original plan was to transform Docks Inc. into a turn-key subcontracting firm. In my time with my previous employer, I had begun creating a need in the industry for this sort of firm, and here's what I mean:

There are all sorts of delays, headaches, and hassles associated with ship repair, in part because it involves so many different trades working on a boat and coordinating with them all. When I managed the project on the mini carrier, I developed the use of "tiger teams" to help solve the coordination problem, and it was a big success. Later on, however, I figured out that I could do one better.

In construction they have what is called a "general contractor." He's the guy that you hire to be responsible for coordinating the plumber, the drywall guys, the electricians, etc. The reason why this works is because A) He has his team of tradesmen that he is familiar with and works with regularly (sort of like a tiger team) and B) He bids the job himself, and his profitability is dependent upon him delivering the job in a timely manner. So instead of me making a million calls to different trade companies, the general contractor's full-time endeavor is whipping the subs into line. He makes money and he assumes the responsibility.

Now, I had nothing to do with the advent of general contractors, but in the ship repair industry, no one had ever followed that model. So I began writing subcontracts this way, searching for craftsmen to bid the whole job, take the responsibility of keeping the subs in line, etc. And slowly, just like with the tiger teams, the rest of the industry began looking for people who would work with them this way. Instead of general contractors, we called them "turn-key contractors."

I had spent a few years creating a need for this sort of company in my industry, and part of my master plan in jumping ship and tying to Docks Inc. was to turn them into a turn-key solution that was now in such high demand and short supply.

Our revenue quadrupled.

# Chapter 26

I was playing the long game.

When I started making real money, I didn't go out and buy a Ferrari. I didn't blow it every week at the card tables. I wanted to climb higher, and that meant putting my money to work for me. I didn't want to buy pleasures that would depreciate or vanish completely. I didn't want to hoard it all and watch as the inflation rate devalued all my hard work. I wanted to invest it and to grow it.

If you grow a crop of potatoes, you can dig them up and eat them when they're ready, or you can dig them up, split them, and plant for an exponential harvest next year. This is what we call the principle of delayed gratification. I can get more later if I sacrifice now.

So I was looking for investments, but investments inherently involve risk. Don't misunderstand me, I do play the stock market a bit these days, in what I hope is an informed manner. But the problem with buying stocks or bonds is that it is entirely predictive, and the decision makers who will increase or decrease the value of my investments really don't have any interaction with me. I exert no influence on them. In many cases, just going out and buying stocks is little better than gambling.

On the other hand, after saving Docks Inc. from bankruptcy, I was a minority shareholder. I had equity in the company that I was helping to run. I knew every detail of my future plans for the firm, I knew my track record (quadrupled the revenue in a short time), I had seen the financials, and I knew the industry. So, when it came time to invest and place a bet, I bet on me.

Here's what I mean – we were not a publically traded company. That means you couldn't just up and buy stock in

Docks Inc.; we were a privately-owned organization, and equity was only owned by so many people. So, whenever I'd save up a bit, I would go to one of my partners, negotiate a deal, and buy their stake in the company. Then, when I'd saved up again, I'd find another partner, and buy him out too. This was my modus operandi for twelve years, and by the end of it, I was one of only three majority shareholders in the company, with 33 percent ownership. My vote made or broke decisions on where to take the company.

And business was good. We had come from earning about a half-million dollars in revenue every year to paying a half-million dollars every *week* in payroll. We went from thirty employees to several hundred in three states. It got so big that it started stretching what we as individuals could do.

It was exciting, gratifying, and tremendously satisfying to be at the helm of so great a success.

I ran a few other ventures on the side as well. Having proven that I could save a business, I figured I could start one as well, so I had a few different partners over these years who went in on deals with me.

Our first venture in the world of entrepreneurialism was a burger and fries type of café inside of another establishment. This lasted less than a year, and I got out of it for various reasons. The second was another short-lived investment called "Homer's Tavern." It was a little bar that did well enough, but the other partners wanted each of us to take shifts behind the counter, and I learned very quickly that the hospitality industry and I do not mix – at least not with me in the front of the house. You see, I had grown accustomed to giving orders. Customers don't like that very much.

Both of those early efforts went fine. No spectacular

successes, but I didn't lose anything either, and I made a little money. The next two were substantially more lucrative. The first was a real estate company I started with my old pal Fitz (who I used to go to Chuey's with) and a contractor named Elliot. We were riding the rising bubble of California real estate for a few years, buying houses, fixing them up in a month or two, then flipping them for substantially more than we had paid. It was good work for a while.

While this was going on, I decided to take one more stab at the hospitality industry by opening up a wine bar in Hillcrest, San Diego. At the time, wine was just starting to really gain popularity, but there were only three other wine bars in all of San Diego County. So, we opened up a swanky wine bar, got rave reviews, and people came in spending their real estate money like they didn't know what to do with it. And this was successful for a few years, but there were a couple of factors that began to make me suspect it was time to abandon the venture.

First, after four or five years, we were no longer the only game in town, nor the coolest. Wine bars sprang up all over the place, and they had upped the level of competition substantially, offering little bistros and five-star chefs doing amuse bouche menus (This is a fancy way of saying, "tiny, expensive food"). We were looking at needing to renew our five-year lease on our wine bar's location, but one other thing gave me pause.

The real estate company was still in full swing, and the revenue was good – too good. The last job we ever did was a little house on Talmadge that we bought. We got it for just below market value at about $400,000. As always, Fitz and I did the demo, then Elliot took the lead on the buildout. After the short period of time it took us to reno-vate, we put the house on the market for $700,000. There was a bidding war, and it ended up selling for $800,000.

That's right, it had doubled in value in just a short period of time.

So, on the one hand we were happy with our fortune, but on the other hand, I knew that this was a sign of an extremely unstable market. The bubble was going to pop, and soon. So, my partners and I agreed this would be our last house. And likewise, in view of the fact that the wine bar's location was costing $21,000 a month to rent, my other partner and I declined to renew the lease, thinking that a real estate crash was likely, which would have meant declining revenue for our luxury bar.

But I wasn't worried. Docks Inc. was my main effort anyway, and that was going stronger than ever, with nothing but blue skies in the forecast.

And then 2007 happened.

As I'm sure everyone reading this will recall, the financial collapse of 2007-2008, also known as the Great Recession, was devastating. The government had been forcing financial institutions to give out bad loans for years, and then the financial institutions, wanting to get rid of these bad investments, packaged them up and tried to make them appealing so that investors would buy their debt, and at a certain point, the market just couldn't bear all of the defaults, foreclosures, and toxic assets imploding. The economy crashed hard, and the banks slammed their doors shut as far as lending goes.

So, on the one hand, I'd come out of my side ventures at just the right time. The guy who rented the space our wine bar used to occupy went out of business trying to pay the rent. There just wasn't enough business anymore, and if we had renewed that lease, it would have bankrupted us as well – and if my real estate buddies and I had continued flipping houses, we would have gotten stuck with some property in the neighborhood of seven figures and with no way of selling. That, too, could have ruined us.

So, with business as with most things, knowing when to get out is just as important as knowing to when to get in. We had survived these side businesses and even done well, but the economy at large was devastated, and that always has consequences, especially when no one is loaning to anybody. I may have been out of my entrepreneur adventures, but I still had Docks Inc. to think about, and all of a sudden we were in a terrible spot.

Here was the issue for Docks Inc.

We had a half-million-dollar payroll to send out every single week. Our company was very profitable and successful, but we weren't selling widgets at the convenience store; we were doing months-long, sometimes years-long projects for the United States government, and payment was often delayed several months or years. In the meantime, that half a million in expenditures starts to add up quick, to say nothing of materials needed for jobs and other expenses. A steady line of credit is what makes large-scale operations like ours possible in a civil society.

So all of a sudden, my partners and I were paying our several hundred employees out of our own pockets and off of our home equity lines of credit.

This is what we in the business call "a little scary."

I am not overstating our predicament when I say that one or two delayed payments from the navy could have literally left my partners and me bankrupt, with the company in shambles. There were times we sold our receivables to a factoring firm for a couple of points, and even then, some of the deposits only hit hours before the payroll checks did. But we soldiered on through it.

They say that the line between having a lot of guts and having no brains whatsoever is a razor's edge, but it's relative to your frame of reference for what is acceptable. To my partners, for instance, this situation was heart-stopping, the scariest thing they'd ever run up against, probably. For my part, I thought, "If this whole thing folds up like a house of cards, they're not going to put me in jail. They're not going to shoot me. My frame of reference for how bad things can get is eighteen months of solitary, and that's not going to happen. So, what the heck? Let's roll." I still had my kids. I had my freedom. I had a positive attitude. Worrying, wringing my hands, and making hasty decisions weren't going to help at all.

So, we funded our company's operating expenses personally, and we stuck it out. I have to commend my partners for their bravery, because if they hadn't decided to go along with this crazy scheme, I would not have been able to float it alone. We figured that we were in this mess together, and we'd get out of it together too.

It took some time, but the economy got a little better. I was able to borrow some money from a good friend to help cover payroll, and eventually the banks loosened up. We no longer had to put everything on the line just to stay in business. Things were good.

For those of you who have been paying attention, you'll know that it's now time for another crisis of epic proportions.

But before I tell you what it was, I'd like to explain some of my philosophy. Crises are opportunities. I don't mean that in a jaded way, like we should profiteer or do anything unethical. What I mean is that most people are going to lose their cool when something truly unexpected happens. If you keep your head, you can oftentimes get ahead in turbulent times. For instance, more millionaires were made during the Great Depression than at any other comparable length of time in U.S. history. Why? Because when the panic took over, and people were running on the banks and selling all of their stocks for the merest fraction of their worth, the people who refused to panic were buying. Sure, some of those companies that they bought stock in folded up and they lost their investments, but many found a way through, and these investors had bought equity for pennies on the dollar.

So you have to keep your head when things go wrong.

Of course, I learned this lesson in dangerous, (allegedly) illegal situations rather than by a history refresher, but we won't go into too many details here. The point is that my company was about to go into another crisis – this one perhaps even bigger than the Great Recession.

The year was 2011. The government was struggling to pass a budget, and so they passed the Budget Control Act and something called "sequestration." So not only could they not do their primary job as congressmen and congresswomen (deciding how to spend money for the year), what they did get through was nothing but fumes. The immediately looming effect was that the armed forces were about to get gutted, facing a budget reduction of something like 50 percent in the short term. You know who else that affects? Defense contractors like my company, who depend on business from the armed forces. It was looking pretty bad.

So, there we were again, the two other majority partners, me, and our two minority shareholders, having come through the turmoil of 2007-2008 only to face it again. This time, it wasn't a matter of securing a loan, but of our clients being able to continue buying our services at anything resembling comparable rates. Just staying in business was a huge risk, and this time, it was one that we were not willing to make.

The consequences of the Budget Control Act and

sequestration were still some months out, so my partners and I decided to sell while we were ahead. The company was strong, earning well, and running on all cylinders, but the handwriting was on the wall. Turns out, not everyone can read that handwriting.

You see, this was all such an incredibly big mess, that most everyone was banking on congress undoing it – repealing sequestration. There was a super-committee, a lot of chest-puffing and promises, and no one wanted to think of what might happen if this nonsense was actually allowed to take effect. I, considering myself a fairly astute observer of congress for the past couple of decades, thought, "This nonsense is actually going to take effect. This is happening." Time would tell who was right, because most of the experts disagreed with my private assessment.

So, we were able to find an enthusiastic buyer, a mid-level private equity firm run by a former secretary of the Navy from a past presidential administration. We went through all of the rigmarole of a sale, reached an agreement, and after months of work, we were ready to sign it all away.

On December 31st, 2012, my partners and I sold our company, and on January 1st, 2013, sequestration, contrary to everyone's expectations, went into effect.

This is what I affectionately refer to as "a really, really close call."

What mattered was that we had kept our heads and hadn't allowed fear or wishful thinking to control our decisions. Our buyers were left with a hard spot of their own choosing, and I walked away with millions, as did my partners.

We had a two-year agreement with our buyer to run the company for them through the transition period, and it was difficult going for a while. The whole industry was badly shaken, but things worked out alright for me. I was still doing the work that I loved, well compensated for doing so, and all of the headaches and existential risks of owning the firm were now gone.

The firm that bought our company, incidentally, took some blows but managed to survive the storm, but seeing it firsthand made me very glad of the moves that my partners and I had made in selling to them. I had a good relationship with our buyer, so after our two years were up, they invited me to stay on as an executive, and I did so gladly.

I love the work that we do, and I consider myself a patriot. I've pasted our commitment to the armed services on our walls, which is that we will always perform to the highest levels as we go to work every day, knowing that the ships we repair and work on are carrying our men into harm's way. I have the privilege of working with high-functioning, really quality folks who work hard and produce, and I am well-esteemed and regarded as an expert in my field.

This is how a five-time loser got out from under the black cloud of doom, that scarlet letter that says "convict: won't ever succeed in the real world." I looked at my life and saw that my vow for my children's sake was fulfilled. I had gone straight for their sakes, and more than that, I had become a titan of industry.

And then, once again, life went and threw me a curveball.

# Chapter 27

It wasn't a single moment.

There was the first time since going straight that I wasn't worried about paying my tab at the grocery store. There was the name plate that the company had made for me and hung outside of my office. It was first one, then ten, then hundreds of nods of respect in the hall. It was pulling out my calendar and seeing every day filled in with important work to do. It was a random drive down the street when the thought occurred to me that I was an entrepreneur – a real businessman. It was the first time I saw my name in the paper – and not in the "Most Wanted" bulletin.

My rise to the top was not instantaneous. There were some bumps, hard lefts, and difficulties along the way. However, slowly but surely my life turned around. I had material comforts, meaningful work, and accomplishments. My children started turning out to be well-adjusted, productive members of society. I became an esteemed member of the community, serving on boards, chambers of commerce, political campaigns, and heading up projects for public good.

The time came when I had achieved everything that I had aspired to, and let me tell you, it's an odd feeling. It felt good.

For a while.

And then something odd started to happen.

Before, I was on a quest to succeed, to beat my circumstances and then to grow a failing company into a successful one, but... I did that. In fact, the tail was starting to wag the dog, if you get my drift. My company had grown so big, that it no longer felt like something I was building but rather like a gigantic beast I was desperately trying to keep under control. We had offices on the East Coast, the West Coast, and in Hawaii. We had hundreds of employees. My typical workday looked like this:

I'd wake up at 1:30 or 2:00 in the morning, and I'd get into work by 4:00 a.m. at the absolute latest – often earlier. I'd read industry and defense news for an hour, send emails and correspondence for an hour, and then I'd have my 6:00 a.m. meeting with the office manager. This was followed by my 7:00 a.m. meeting with all of the department heads, and then at 8:00 a.m. I had a standing appointment with our attorneys, because some disgruntled employee or contractor was always suing. I won't belabor the rest of the specifics here, because I think you get the idea. It was out of one meeting and into another all day, constantly making decisions and struggling to keep up. I'd get home in the afternoon, pour myself the first glass of Crown Royal whiskey, and start working with the Hawaii operations, where the employees were just getting done with lunch. I'd work until dinner, and then there would always be something else to do. I'd cross off everything I'd done from my to-do list, and everything I hadn't gotten to I would roll over to the next day. I'd fall into bed around 10:00 or 11:00 p.m.

Of course, I was drinking like a fish for the second half of every day, running on adrenaline, nicotine, caffeine, alcohol, and three or four hours of sleep.

Ron, who was sick with pulmonary hypertension and a series of degenerative strokes, told me that he was worried that I was killing myself the way I was living.

When someone who can barely stand up straight, who's as thin as a ghost and operating on a terminal diagnosis tells you that they're worried about your health, it's a little disconcerting.

Business was a great servant but a terrible master. The same goes for money.

But this wasn't all that I had. I also had a stunningly beautiful, Argentinian woman as my wife – and after only a handful of months, the relationship was in shambles. I don't like talking much about my third marriage, so if you're waiting for more details, don't hold your breath.

And, to top it off, despite the RV in the driveway, the beautiful house, the corporate influence, and the wealth at my disposal, I couldn't make my best friend Ron any better from his sickness. He was getting worse, and there was nothing I could do about it.

I had achieved everything I could have ever hoped for, and I even had the trophy wife who was supposed to be enjoying it all with me.

But it didn't look like I thought it would. As it turns out, it never does.

Let me assure you – nobody wants to reach the top of a mountain they've been climbing for twenty years and say, "That's it?" I tried to convince myself that I was happy and the discontent was just from not getting enough sleep, or wanting to finish this or that contract, but it wasn't true. All of the things I had sought, that I thought would bring me satisfaction and meaning did not. I actually hated all of the things that I thought would bring me happiness. I still had problems, and paradise didn't look so grand from inside the gates.

This may sound like "first world problems" to you, but remember that I've lived on the other side as well. I know what it's like to live on government cheese, to be cold, lonely, abused, and poor. And when I became a millionaire, something that I thought would solve everything, I found out that managing that money is a responsibility. If you don't watch it, it'll vanish, eaten up by careless spending, bad investments, or even just inflation and disuse. Don't get me wrong, I'd rather have money than not have it, but it isn't going to rock me to sleep at night. It isn't going to hold my hand and offer me sympathy when I'm going through a hard time. It is another responsibility to take care of.

And I was up to my eyeballs in responsibility.

Once I was safe, my kids were safe, and there were no more mountains to climb, there was enough space for me to see that there was sort of a vanity and an aimlessness to it all.

This jumble of thoughts was all summed up in that one question that wouldn't leave my mind:

"This can't be it, right?"

# Chapter 28

Whoever said that alcohol impairs your ability to make decisions didn't get it quite right. When I used to drink, I'd make all *kinds* of decisions. Alcohol impairs your ability to make *good* decisions, or decisions that you would normally want to make if sober.

And that's how I ended up going to church.

Bear with me.

It was a Saturday night, and I thought I'd get together with a buddy of mine named Jay. Now, the first thing you need to know about Jay is that he is big. I am not one to be intimidated by the stature of anyone, but let's just say that Jay's size makes a good argument.

Anyway, Jay is a great guy and a friend of mind. He's a motorcycle cop, so in a weird way we have a lot in common. He and I were down the street from my house at a little bar called Jamacha Junction. (Just for the record, no, I did not misspell "Jamaica." Jamacha is the most mispronounced and head-scratching street name in all of San Diego. It sounds like "ham-a-shaw.") So, Jay and I were having a good time, solving the world's problems at the local watering hole, as it were. And I don't know what made Jay think this was a good opportunity, but he says to me, "Hey, Flash, why don't you go to church with me in the morning?"

Under any other circumstance, I would have stifled a chuckle and politely said, "No." Church was not for me. It wasn't that the me-and-church dynamic was like oil and water, it was more like the fish-bicycle dynamic: It didn't exist. Church and I existed in separate realities. I didn't think about religion, God, or any of that. I certainly didn't want to think about any of it. It was irrelevant to me, and the thought of spending an hour or two of my precious time at some stuffy Christian institution simply did not compute.

So, when Jay asked me to go to church with him, I raised my glass and said, "Sure! Why not?"

I was fairly liquored up by the time he asked me. He probably could have asked me to wear a ninja turtle costume and juggle bowling pins, and I might've said yes. Needless to say, I immediately forgot about what I had agreed to. I didn't really know what I was saying at that point.

Jay, it seems, was not as oiled up as I had been, because the next morning as I was lying in bed, I heard a second set of banging. There was already the banging in my head, but suddenly there was more banging, and it wouldn't stop. So I finally got up and shuffled to my door, where lo and behold, there's Jay dressed in his Sunday best telling me that I'm going to church with him.

I had no idea what was going on, but like I said before – Jay's a big guy. I was in no mood to get into an argument or altercation with someone like Jay, considering the massive headache that I had. I was quite reluctant, but I agreed, mostly to get the noise to stop.

## Church for the Broken

So, that's how I ended up sitting in Skyline Church with a hangover and no idea of what I was doing there. But after the music and worship was over, the pastor took the stage, and something happened.

It was like the sermon had been written just for me, entirely for my benefit and circumstance. The preacher gave a message all about simplifying your life, and it was exactly what I needed to hear.

My life at that point was controlled chaos at best. I had no space. If it wasn't work, it was community efforts or some other endeavor. There I was day after day, juggling all this stuff, and I couldn't even see past the end of my nose half the time. I was constantly at peak capacity, and I was on the verge of burnout.

The clear takeaway from the day was to simplify my life, and the preacher gave some tips to help me do just that.

So, the sermon really resonated with me, which I found surprising. I didn't think a sermon could have practical value, but there it was. Going to service that first week helped me so much that I figured it was a good place to get some advice, and so I went the next week, and then the one after that, too. Eventually, I started attending regularly with my good buddy Jay.

It wasn't all just practical advice. They spent a lot of time talking about the Bible and an ancient Jewish Rabbi named Jesus, who was God in human form. There was talk of "sin" and "virtue," "eternal consequences" and the "kingdom of God." It was like describing thermonuclear energy to a cat. I had never really heard about these things before, and to be perfectly honest, the people I had known to be the most vocally Christian throughout my life were… a little strange.

But I knew one thing and I knew it firmly: My own plans had not succeeded in producing contentment, peace, or satisfaction in my life. I felt hollow, and it wasn't just because of the bad relationship or the busy schedule. I was in a place where I really wanted to know if there was a point to this cosmic rodeo or not. The church crowd said that God had a plan and a purpose for me. I didn't know if it was true, but I figured I'd give them a fair hearing.

Regularly going to church led to a mentor who wanted to walk me through the spiritual side of my life, which I

was now paying attention to for the first time in my life.
His name was Paul Rischer.

# Chapter 29

Paul Risher was the "integration pastor" at Skyline, and I figured that meant he was responsible for integrating sinners like me into the community of saints that everyone else seemed to be.

It was not a seamless process. I had a lot of questions, difficulties, and conflicts in my mind that took a while to figure out.

Thankfully, Paul is what I would describe as a prince of a man. He's a saint in the true sense of the word, very patient and kind.

Paul and I would go to lunch and talk about faith and God, and he slowly taught me what it meant to be a Christian. You see, that first Sunday at church, the lead pastor preached like he was talking to me and only me. However, in the following weeks, it wasn't like that. He was an accomplished theologian and scholar, and his tendency was to speak to the already initiated, those mature in the faith. He used jargon that I didn't understand – Christian-ese, they call it. It was like we were on separate planets sometimes.

But then Paul would break it down for me later, and I'd have the chance to discuss the topics at hand and work through them. He really took time on this old sinner, and I was spoon-fed the faith, which was a necessity for me.

## Stumbling Blocks

You see, I had a number of blocks keeping me from committing to God. For one thing, I really, truly did not want to be a hypocrite. I'd spent half of my life lying, cheating, and allegedly doing all sorts of worse crimes. Sure,

I had turned a new leaf and gained respectability, but in my mind, I was still that rebel and lost soul. I'd been prominent in the criminal underworld, and now I was going to waltz into church every week like I belonged? It smelled like dishonesty, and I wasn't sure that I ought to put on a front like that.

And then Paul went and ruined that defense for me.

He explained that everyone is a hypocrite. Everyone is doubleminded in some way or another. We all act in ways contrary to what we say that we believe because every single person has that battle in their hearts between living on the dark side or the light. Dressing up, greeting people with a smile, and going to church wasn't a proclamation that I was somehow perfect; it was an honest effort to be something better. To live in the light. Effort towards change doesn't make you a hypocrite; pretending that you have no need for change is what does it.

Well, that's all well and good, and in a way it lined up with my second vow in my life that I would go straight for my kids' sake. When I made that change, I wasn't pretending to be anything different than I was, I was switching directions because I needed to and because it was right. I wore a suit and tie because it was respectable, but I knew that underneath it all, I still had all the prison tattoos to remind me of my past.

That led me to another stumbling block. It took me a bit to admit it, but every time I walked through the sanctuary doors, I half expected them to catch fire or get struck by lightning on account of the hellion I'd been. I figured my presence profaned the place, offended God, and I'd be better off hiding from Him and staying off His radar. But, as I knew from my tenure in business, "hiding and hoping it goes away" is pretty much always a bad strategy that blows up in your face. Better to deal with things head on.

Paul told me the hard truth that, yes, my past did offend God. God is holy, and He hates the sorts of things that I had done. But God is able to love perfectly even in my own failure and brokenness. You see, I'd look in the mirror and see the tattoos under my business clothes. God looked at the tattoos and saw a deeper layer – my heart – that He could clean and make new. It was just a matter of being upfront with the Big Guy Upstairs, owning up to my dirt, and letting Him call the shots from here on out.

Evidently, God is patient. He takes a long time to get angry. You definitely don't want Him angry at you, but if we own up to our junk and come to Him humbly, we find His grace instead of His wrath.

Most of my barriers to finding Christ were just out of ignorance. When you spend a good part of your life not even remotely considering religion and, in fact, representing everything that is wrong in the world, the way you think and breathe is foreign to God's truth. And that was me for a long time. I just couldn't wrap my head around it all.

And I have to say that part of the reason I didn't want to commit was because, for most of my life, I only knew of one kind of Christian. I want to put this delicately, but some believers are what I would affectionately refer to as "zealous." They really wear their faith on their sleeve. "Father," "kingdom," "spirit," and "heaven" account for eighty-five percent of all the words that come out of their mouths, and they can be very aggressive and in your face. These people are passionate about what they believe, and God bless them for that. I'm sure a lot of good comes from their tenacity, but sometimes, to me, it just feels like too much. And when I started my faith journey, the only picture of Christians I had in my head was these folks.

These sincere, but often obnoxious and socially oblivious, folks. I thought, "That can't be what I want to be, right? Someone you can't even have a conversation with?"

A short time around church helped me get over that one. Not everyone wears their faith on their sleeve. A lot of good, faithful people go to work every day and live their faith, sharing truth and wisdom when there's opportunity, and living like healthy, normal, loving people.

This is not to say that you shouldn't get "too into" God or anything like that. God's out there asking for a full commitment. It is, however, saying that maybe we should not hyperventilate while we're talking to people. Maybe we should care about them enough to want to know who they are and listen to them talk a little bit too, instead of only ever being willing to talk about what we want to talk about.

Paul was one of these reasonable, faithful Christians. Getting to know him and others like him made me want to be a Christian too.

Hindsight being twenty-twenty, all of these stumbling blocks were affected by the fact that I didn't believe yet. Once you believe, it's easier to see the truth of it all, somehow, and the whole thing fits together. If you don't believe, you're conflicted because you're still straddling the fence.

## Assignments

So, as you can imagine, I had a lot of questions. And Paul would patiently walk me through what the Bible says, and he'd answer whatever I brought to him. He gave me assignments too, sort of like homework for the spiritual seeker. This looked like reading parts of the Bible or other books, and he'd introduce me to situational awareness through scripture. I would tell him, "Hey, I've got this thing going on in my life," and he would explain, "This is what happened in the Bible. Let's talk about why it's relevant."

Paul is a great man, and in dealing with me, he had the patience of Job. He even had that patience in his own life, because, tragically, he lost his wife shortly after our mentoring sessions ended. She was diagnosed with a vicious disease that was degenerative, and so for three years she declined, and he took care of her and mourned all the while. But that was some time ago now, and he's remarried and seems to be happy. He exemplified the perseverance and faithfulness in his own life, even when God handed him hard things, so when he spoke to me, he had authority. In the old days, I would have said he had "street cred."

I never would have made it far without Paul, and his mentoring was to help me out a lot in the future.

### Sink or Swim

I've said it before and I'll say it again; if you go into a barber shop enough times, you're going to get a haircut. In this case, that was a positive thing. Regularly going to church and meeting with Paul taught me a lot about who God is and why He was interested in me at all. Paul led me through that sinner's prayer where you tell God that you're sorry for all of the things you've done wrong in your life and that you believe in Him and what Jesus did on that cross. Then, you ask Him into your heart and offer to live your life for God. Later, I even invited a few friends to watch me get baptized by Lindo Lake at the community center.

I got the haircut.

The irony of my circumstances did not elude me. Most of the time it seems like people find Jesus in jail, at rock bottom, at their lowest point. Me, I was too hard-headed for that. When I was in prison I was proud of the fact. It was part of the life I'd chosen, and I wasn't about to let some pain and discomfort make me think I needed anybody else. I wasn't afraid of anyone, remember? It wasn't until I had it all that I realized I really had nothing. And that is the rock that started to break my pride, and led to the third and final vow of my life:

"I will live the rest of my life for God."

Of course, at the time I made it, I had absolutely no idea what this vow meant. I realize that may detract from the gravity of this moment, but it's the honest truth. When I gave the Lord my life, it was less from a well-reasoned and carefully considered dedication and more from an attitude of, "Why not? I've tried everything else. Maybe this will stick."

You see, alcohol is fun and games for a while, but the buzz loses its appeal eventually. Chasing women didn't fill my need for meaning. My third marriage was so bad that even Paul was telling me to divorce her. Success in business was a genuinely good thing, but it was like the more I leaned on it to satisfy me, the less that it actually did. I was up for most anything at this point, and I'd seen how the church could help my thinking and my life.

I still had a long road to go until I found something that tastes like true faith, but I believe that God in His mercy and kindness can honor what I affectionately call a "broken hallelujah." My initial conversion was flawed, if mostly sincere.

And it was a good thing, too, because something truly terrible was about to happen.

# Chapter 30

All things considered, my break with the old life was a clean one. Sure, I had to go through another divorce, putting an endcap on a marriage that had lasted less than a year, but my kids were good, work was going well (and less stressful than before). I was a man in good standing with the law, and I'd even started to explore the deeper questions in life.

I'd outrun most of my demons, and it didn't seem to me that they were catching up any time soon. But others weren't so lucky.

Ron and I had always been close, and it was nice to have a friend to ride to work with after Tom died. My kids loved hanging out with "Uncle Ron," and I learned a lot from him. For a bizarre, messed-up family situation, it wasn't so bad. But Ron had come from the dark side, too, and his demons followed a little closer.

He had made a clean break in so far as running up against the law was concerned. Ron had turned a new leaf and proven that his change of heart was sincere, but consequences are a funny thing. Rub up against some poison oak, and a lot of times you aren't going to see a rash crop up until a week later. Evil things are like that sometimes: Delayed.

Ron had a history of using methamphetamine, and that sort of history doesn't just go away, even if you stop using.

It gets to your heart and lungs in a bad way, first of all. Heart failure, toxicity, irregular heartbeats, strokes, intense vasoconstriction of the pulmonary arteries, and organ failure are just some of the medical jargon we can apply to those who use meth for a prolonged period of time.

It affects your brain, of course. The rapid high that meth offers comes at a cost — namely that the body's regulatory systems can get all out of whack, which messes up your ability to think straight. It takes some years to get back to where you can be alright, relaxed, and clear-headed, but there are other effects that are harder to heal.

In Ron's case, he was getting sicker and sicker, and they diagnosed him with pulmonary hypertension. Hypertension brought blood clots, and blood clots brought blood thinners, which was incidentally why Ron had to quit the motorcycle club in the first place. He found out what any sort of traumatic wound, especially a motorcycle crash, would do to somebody on blood thinners. Then his troubles started, first with an irregular heartbeat, then with little strokes that got bigger and more debilitating every time they struck.

This substance that Ron had partaken of so habitually in the past in order to bring quick pleasure now brought him only pain and decay.

Meth's a hell of a drug. It's evil. The only reason I wasn't in the same boat as Ron was because I kept getting incarcerated during the heyday of meth. I was never out long enough to do it for long enough to develop the sorts of complications that started wreaking havoc on him. And wreaking havoc was exactly what it did.

As Ron got worse, he had to take on less at work. Then, he wasn't able to work at all. Soon, after a particularly bad stroke, he was no longer ambulatory and his speech was impacted, his brain shutting down bit by bit. He couldn't talk to people on the phone, and he'd get so frustrated just trying to do the simplest things. While he could still walk, I remember coming home, and I'd often see that he'd been pacing on his doorstep for hours, waiting for me to come around so I could help him with some little task that he just couldn't accomplish.

I took care of him while he was down and out. I

cooked all of his meals, helped him through all the essentials of everyday living. I was basically his nurse, and though that is not a role I would generally see myself in, for Ron, my friend, I would do whatever it took.

His downhill slide was fast. The doctors told him that there was nothing they could do to stop the continuing nerve damage. Since he was terminal, they brought in hospice, who fixed him up with whatever painkillers and comforts that he wanted.

Ron didn't want any of that. He wanted his mind back. He wanted to be able to work and to use his body again, but that wasn't going to happen.

In the end, he decided to take himself out. Hospice provides plenty of drugs, and in lethal doses, so Ron used what ability he had left to take his own life.

I saw him before he slipped away. The bottle was still on the table, almost empty from the deliberate overdose. He told me that he didn't want to live anymore, but he said he did not want to talk about it or he would start to cry. I was grateful for that much at least, because it was all I could do to keep from crying too. I stumbled through leading him in whatever prayers of forgiveness and salvation that I knew, barely keeping it together. I held Ron in my arms, then, and he died.

November 1st, 2009 was one of the worst days of my life. Ron was more than a friend; he was a brother.

It wasn't the first time something like this had happened to me. Several years earlier, when I was still on the wrong side of the law, an old biker pal named Animal got into the same sort of mess as Ron. He had developed renal cell carcinoma from cooking meth. Back in those days, it wasn't exactly laboratory conditions that were used to manufacture the drug. He had sustained a back injury years before from a hang-gliding accident, and so when the cancer started, he thought it was just more back pain. By the time he knew something was really wrong, it had spread from his kidneys and wrapped around his spine. He was in constant pain, and the doctors told him that all they could do as he marched toward his day of reckoning was sever the nerves. He took himself out, and I had the mixed blessing of being able to see him just before he died.

Sometimes it feels like death has followed me around, taunting me. There were plenty of times that I should have died in the old days, but I never did. And yet, just to show that I am a powerless mortal in this bigger game of life, I've seen many friends pass on before their time. I held Tom, Ron, and Animal as they slipped away. How many people can say that by the time they're forty years old? These weren't old men, and we weren't on a battlefield during a war.

I guess you could say I had some survivor's guilt. I did my best to carry on, but inside, my heart was dark for a long time. It was a heavy load to carry.

Now, I understand that everyone makes his or her own choices, and I suppose we'll all stand before God to explain ourselves one day. But just for the sake of being clear to my readers out there, I do not think that suicide is a proper response to pain or hardship. I think there's always hope as long as you're breathing, and the better thing to do is fight it to the final round.

I miss my friends. God help me, even now, I miss them.

# Chapter 31

Ron's decline and death were difficult, but one good thing came out of that time, at least.

As his condition worsened, I knew that he was going to need some in-home medical care, at minimum for the time while I was at work. So, seeing as how my neighbor was a medical assistant, I asked her to come by one day and tell me what she thought about Ron's situation. She came over, and she brought her friend who was also a medical assistant.

Her friend was named Lyndy.

I think that we sensed from the beginning that we were kindred spirits. She was (and is) beautiful, of course – fair hair and warm eyes. But what really stood out to me was that she and I were cut from the same cloth, pilgrims walking the same road. Lyndy was a recovered heroin addict, and she'd done a couple of terms in jail. Now here she was trying to walk the straight and narrow and make something out of her life.

This was appealing to me. Going to prison changes you, and it's hard for people to understand that. Being an addict of any kind does things to you, and even when you are well, you have these roots that you're never going to forget. Suddenly, all these years into my new life, here was a woman who really understood me and related to who I was and what I was trying to do.

She even went to church, which was still a new thing for me, but definitely a plus.

So, after that first day, talking over what Ron's needs would be, Lyndy and I started hanging out. We'd go out to a bar and play pool and have a few drinks. Both of us were still drinking a bit back then. I would have her over and barbeque or cook her a fancy dinner. Her mom was a really wonderful lady, and so she was around for a lot of our dates at the beginning because, hey, we weren't teenagers anymore, and why leave out a sweet woman whose company we enjoy? Lyndy came from a big family, and family was important to her, so we made accommodations.

So there I was, trying to learn how to fulfill the final vow of my life, to live the rest of my days for God, and this woman appeared who understood me, who liked to have a good time, and was dead set on making things better.

I don't know if this was a reward from heaven or an angel sent to help me on the way, but growing close to Lyndy helped to heal my heart – and not all relationships do that, let me tell you. I don't just mean that it was redemption for bad relationships in the past; something about the way she was predisposed to think, react, and make decisions was just godly. She had her demons and struggles too, just like we all do, but here was the most selfless relationship I'd ever been a part of.

Lyndy is more concerned with my happiness and well-being than with what she wants. In turn, I am more concerned about her desires and well-being than with my own needs. The sum total of it is that we both make each other happy, and I think there is something spiritual about that, which we ought to live out in other parts of our lives too.

I asked her to marry me after a while. She said no.

She had been down that road before, just like me, and it's easy to get cynical about the whole institution. Besides, she was recovering from some struggles of her own, was trying to finish her schooling and medical certifications, and she just didn't want to do it.

It mattered to me, however. I may have been a five-time loser in the eyes of the law, but here I was after years of perseverance a successful businessman and respected citizen. So even though I was a three-time loser at marriage, I knew that there was still a chance for doing it right at long last.

After Ron passed, I asked her again, and she was ready this time. She said yes.

If you're looking for a grandiose, romantic story about planes writing messages in the clouds and rooms filled with rose petals, read something else. I wasn't an idealistic sixteen-year-old asking my date to prom, and I sure wasn't some twenty-year-old kid asking a girl to marry him against a backdrop of the sunset and the Mormon Tabernacle Choir. Lyndy and I had been beaten up by the world a little bit, often at our own doing, and more than excitement, spectacle, or fireworks, going to that courthouse with Lyndy and her family felt like a relief.

This was a part of my life I'd always struggled with and failed at, and finally we were onto something good.

# Chapter 32

I started to get frustrated with the whole church thing.

Paul Rischer, the integration pastor, was a gem, and he showed real kindness to me. The church helped me a lot. But when I started coming around, they were in the midst of a building campaign, and I began to get irritated with how many times I was getting tapped for a building offering.

Now, I'm a businessman, and I understand that things cost money. I understand the need to fundraise and be persistent. But it was so much and so often that it started to really sit wrong with me. There was the regular building offering, a faith offering – it got to the point where it seemed like, "Uh, you. Today is blue shirt guy offering!"

I became weary of it, if I'm being honest. They were mostly good folks, I think. Just pushing too hard to get their sanctuary built.

Since I was experiencing some frustration at my church of origin, Lyndy asked me if I'd like to go to church with her and her family at a place that we'll just call "Ecclesia." She told me that they had a great pastor who was a really gifted speaker, and since he targeted his talks to the layman, I might find it a better fit.

I was up for a change, so that's how I landed at Ecclesia, and Lyndy was as good as her word. The people were warm and generous, and the lead pastor was captivating.

## The Perfect Place for Imperfect People

I remember the first time I met the lead pastor at Ecclesia, whom we'll refer to as "Rusty." We were at some welcome barbeque or something, and someone introduced me to him. I don't remember what we talked about or if it was anything profound, but what I do remember was that he was engaging, a true force of personality. When Rusty looks at you, it's like you have the totality of his attention. He's a smart guy with an illustrious career behind him, and it was easy to feel like you were friends the moment you met him.

He didn't seem holier-than-thou, which was part of the draw for me. Ecclesia made a point of it to seek out the rough-around-the-edges crowd. Let's just say I was far from the only ex-biker at church. Rusty's motto was "no perfect people allowed," and that was a mantra that I and the other members of Ecclesia really resonated with. Life is messed up and complicated, beautiful and stupid, full of mistakes, lucky breaks, and sharp left turns. What matters is that the church was there to come alongside you on the way and point you back to God.

I met a lot of other great people there as well. The executive pastor, Clint Morgan, was the other half of the dynamic duo that made up the core of the church. Clint took care of the contracts, securing a location, coordinating volunteers, financial stuff, etc. and Rusty was the show pony, who did the preaching and served as the face of Ecclesia. And he really was incredible.

Rusty's sermons were dynamic, helpful, and the way he preached was just different. He broke things down and made them easy for me to understand, not having come from a church background. I remember one time he was doing a sermon series on sex, and he had them set out a big old mattress and headboard on the stage, and he was play-acting this little back and forth with an imaginary spouse off-stage, where he kept bringing up things like, "Did you clip your toenails?" and all those sorts of things that generally throw ice water on that kind of situation. He was funny.

I met the elders and the people on the board, all of whom just had your best interests at heart. It was a beautiful community, and it made me glad to be part of it. So I committed to Ecclesia church 100 percent.

I tithed, I served, I volunteered. I ran the entire security team (and our security was *good*). Clint, the executive pastor, became a close friend, and he was the one who baptized me. I became one of the top 5 percent of donors, invested in their building campaign, and I was plugged in to all of the comings and goings of church operations. I made this place my home, and for a short time, it was wonderful.

We'd volunteer thirty hours a week, easily, and for a guy with the sort of work schedule that I had, believe me — that's dedication. Sundays were a big day. We rented a out a school on the weekends, so every Sunday morning we had to haul in, unload, and set up everything, and then after three services we had to tear down, reload, and haul it all off again. Plus, we had meetings, vision-casting, fundraisers, and on and on and on. But I didn't mind the time and the sweat. We had a mission. We were a church. Rusty hadn't come from the same background as a lot of us, but he was one of us. He was our fearless leader, and we would have followed him to hell and back with smiles on our faces.

Imagine that: Marcel Becker, a church man. Strangely, it felt good.

After the scandal, the split, and the fallout, however, it suddenly didn't feel so good.

## Testing

This church that had taken me in, that I had invested so much of myself into, where Rusty spoke to me on a weekly basis as a friend and a guide, teaching me about the Bible, had an imbroglio.

You see, Rusty was an ambitious man. He had great vision, great rhetoric, and a great, big head on his shoulders. He wanted to do a lot of good things, but you'd better believe that if he was set on doing something, it was his way or the highway, and that's all there was to it. This became a problem.

Rusty and his wife decided to adopt a child. They had already had a few kids of their own, and they graciously wanted to provide a home for someone less fortunate. Unfortunately, this country's adoption laws make the process extremely difficult, tiresome, and, most of all, expensive. It was a strain on his pocketbook, I think. I know that I personally had given him some money to help with his adoption lawyer's fees, as had others at the church. I imagine this, at the beginning, was where Rusty came up with his hair-brained scheme that was destined to rip the church apart.

Why sugarcoat it? He wanted a bigger salary.

Rusty was keen on keeping track of who was tithing and who wasn't, schmoozing the big donors, etc., but the thing of it was that we just weren't that established of a church. We'd only been running a few years, and we had about four hundred congregants, many of whom were recently out of prison or gangs, so many people either couldn't or didn't give money to the church. Rusty made a fair salary for his position as lead pastor – I'd guess it was eighty or ninety thousand – but he decided that he needed a lot more.

And hey, I'm not one to judge at this point in the story. California is expensive, adopting is expensive, and when you're providing for a household of five or six, you need to be bringing home the bacon. What I, and most of the rest of Ecclesia had a problem with, was his method of increasing his salary.

Rusty told the board that he wanted to fire Clint, his friend, executive pastor, and advisor who had left his thriving business to take a severe pay cut and help Rusty start this church. Needless to say, Rusty's proposal alienated and angered Clint, and it made the rest of the board pretty unhappy as well.

In a less-than-artful show of force, Rusty rolled over the board's disagreement, made the call anyway, and booted out Clint, saying that he would absorb his responsibilities and his salary. So, take what he was making already, add Clint's sixty-or seventy-thousand-dollar salary to it, and he figured that was a great idea.

For those of you unfamiliar with the vagaries of business and finance, doubling your own salary in a day at the expense of another executive is not something that is generally done, and in a church of four hundred, paying a lead pastor one hundred fifty grand did not seem prudent. The elders were understandably upset, as was Clint, who, as a thank-you for leaving his lucrative business to come and labor at the church, was shown the door.

What do you think happened? Clint (forcibly) resigned, and most of the elders followed suit, albeit by their own volition.

I wasn't on the board, but I knew Clint and the others quite well, so I was aware of what had happened.

It hurt me, and it was difficult, but life is rough sometimes, right? I was conflicted because I was committed to Ecclesia, but that all changed with one phone call.

Rusty called me up and lied to me with a straight face about what had happened. I'm sure he gave me the party line – what everyone had agreed on being the "public statement," you know – but it didn't remotely resemble the truth. You know what he told me?

"Yeah, I have some tough news. Clint's really wanting to get into business, and so he wants to resign his position here. He wants to retire and pursue other opportunities."

It was pure BS. Clint had given up all those "other opportunities" to serve the church; he had resigned without having any other options due to Rusty making a money grab.

Hearing the lie upset me so much that I wanted to vomit.

First of all, I was thinking, "You don't have to lie to me. I'm on your side, and I'll back you through a tough spot." Secondly, I was thinking, "I already know the truth." Loyalty matters to me, and this felt like as clear a violation as I'd seen. I loved and respected Rusty. I would have killed for him. And yet he called me up and lied to me in order to keep me donating.

I was very angry.

So, in the fallout of the resignations, the truth came out just a few days later. Half of the church split off, the biggest donors left, and Ecclesia fell on hard times. As for me, I left the church, but I didn't find another one. I'd been burned, and I wasn't eager to repeat the experience.

Rusty ended up moving off to another church run by a relative of his, and eventually he took over. I suppose all people make mistakes and hopefully they do better in the future, but this one was hard for me.

Rusty was supposed to be the one setting the bar for the rest of us. He was supposed to be leading the way, showing us how we ought to live, work, and behave. He was the one who was there to help us find God.

He might as well have spit in my face.

So, I stopped going to church. And in retrospect, that turned out to be a very, very bad decision.

# Chapter 33

You know, God doesn't talk to me like I hear some people say He talks to them.

Some people say, "The Lord spoke to me," or "I felt God say," etc. I guess I'm not high enough on the food chain to where He speaks to me on a regular basis. Honestly, maybe He does speak to me and I'm just too thickheaded to get the message or to see the signs. But what I do know is that when I was angry and allowed that anger to push me to leave the Church, God was not pleased.

It's amazing how much easier it is to believe when things are going okay. When you don't have any bitterness in your heart, your eyes are wide open and it's like the truth is just right there in front of you. But when resentment found a home in me, it was like everything clouded over. My vision was distorted, and everything went dark.

The voice of reason in my head was a friend named Mike, who worked for a local congressman. Every time we'd get together, he'd say that I needed to go back to church, that what had happened was one man's sin and I shouldn't get mad at God for it. He told me that everybody falls short at one time or another, so it was time to get over it and find a new church where I could worship God. Although Mike was a strong voice of faith in my ear at that time, I still refused to listen and stayed far away from any church.

I still believed there was a God. I'd had enough near misses and seen enough of the miracle of creation to know that for sure. But everything else I'd come to believe and trust over the short course of my faith journey suddenly seemed unimportant. Maybe it was true, maybe it wasn't. I was mad, and that's what mattered. I had been wronged by someone who was supposed to help me out, so why should I go and stick my neck out again?

This was when I believe that the Lord spoke to me, but He didn't use words. My son Eric was killed in a motorcycle crash on July 12, 2017.

If you haven't lived through it, you cannot imagine that phone call. No one wants to tell a father that their boy is dead. There's something about the hesitation, the timidity of the person on the other end of the line, to where you almost know what they're going to say before they say it. You keep pinching yourself, hoping that it's all a terrible dream, but you're going to wake up from it, right?

But you don't wake up. And slowly it dawns on you that this is real life.

This was four years after I started attending Ecclesia and about a year after I had left the church altogether. And suddenly, with this tragedy of unspeakable proportions happening, I didn't have the church to help me. I didn't have God to pray to. My boy was gone, and I felt so alone.

I thought I'd known heartbreak before. I'd seen my fair share of tragedy and lives cut short. I'd had friends die in my arms on a number of occasions. But when my strong, beautiful son was taken from me, I learned what it meant to have a broken heart.

That's the sort of message that even a thick skull like mine can understand.

I thought, "Marcel, why did you stop going to church? What were you thinking? What, are you going to punish God? Where is Eric now? Have you given up on seeing him again? You're out of line, and you need to re-evaluate this whole stepping away thing."

I don't know if God took my son because I turned my back on Him, or if my son was going to die anyway and

God just used the occasion to remind me how foolish I was to try and walk through this life on my own resources. Either way, I felt deep in my heart that the message was this: "Go back to the faith. You need it. You made a vow."

## Getting Warmer

If you've ever gone out into the snow without gloves on, then tried to warm them up by the heater in your car, you know that the restoration isn't immediate. Getting warm hurts. It's a slow process to drive out the cold. Well, that's what grieving a major loss is like. Grieving is like being numb. Even when you start to heal, it takes time.

But I held onto as much as I knew. Once again, someone close to me was taken too soon, and me – this crass old sinner – had been left behind. Why wasn't I the one in that car accident? Why wasn't I the one dying of neuropathy in an ex-biker buddy's house? Why wasn't I the one who collapsed on the docks with a heart attack? Why, out of all those bullets that flew in my dark days, did none of them take me out?

God seemed to be telling me that He had a use for me. My service wasn't done. I had to go back.

In September, two months after Eric passed away, I picked up the phone and called Clint, the pastor who had baptized me. I told him what had been going on, and I said that I'd like to come back to church and follow God again. I asked him where all of our old friends were attending since the split of Ecclesia, and he told me about a new church that everybody had joined. I wasn't ready quite yet, but I told him that in the New Year, I would come back.

I was still processing it all, trying to lick my wounds and figure out what I was doing. But despite everything, I was as good as my word. The first Sunday of the New Year, I was back in church.

It was an amazing, heartwarming return.

All of the folks I had been so fond of at Ecclesia, the people I had served alongside and known, welcomed me with open arms like it was homecoming. Everyone was just so happy to have me back and to see me, and that is an unusual and wonderful feeling to experience. Everyone asked me where I had disappeared to, told me that they had been worried about me, praying for me, and they offered their condolences about my son. In the midst of it all, I thought, "You know what? I'm in the right spot. I'm doing the right thing."

So, I got dedicated, but this time, I wasn't just dedicated to a church. People fail, pastors lie, and leaders come and go, but the faith is built on Jesus. This time I got dedicated to God.

I started really paying attention to what was going on in this church, the teaching, doctrine, and worship. I went through and watched the sermon series online that I had missed. The guys preaching at this church were young but very sharp. One of them holds a doctorate, and both of them really teach scripture well, out of the New Living Translation, so it's easy for me to understand. What they do is, instead of trying to interpret scripture and put their own spin on it, they just preach what the Bible says and provide you with historical and cultural context so that you can better understand the message.

I just could not get enough. I asked the pastors, "Hey, can you give me some books to read?" On their recommendation, I started reading first century history, learning about the world at the time Jesus was walking around. I read Paul's letters to the Corinthians, a book called *Simply Christian*, and others. I devoured it.

Suddenly, I was healing. Suddenly, I had peace. Even

after the tragedy of losing my son Eric, I had peace.
I was free at last.

# Epilogue

The title of this book means a lot to me. "Free at Last" is appropriate because today, that's how it is for me. I'm not only free from the dark days, I'm free from all of the nonsense that I thought life was supposed to be about – being the corporate titan, being the millionaire and all that. That means nothing to me now. I found out that there is a (very patient) God out there who loves us and has a purpose for us. He even has a purpose for me.

The most important thing I do now is help others who are in a tough spot, experiencing the darkest days of their lives post addiction, post incarceration, thinking that there's no hope for them. I provide them with hope. That's why I tell my story, because when I talk with people who feel like they've messed up their lives beyond repair, that nothing could ever be different, so they might as well keep on in their self-destruction, they get to see one guy who made it out alive:

Me.

I assure you, if I could do it, you can too. You can live well. You can make a change. You can find peace.

Keep in mind that it's going to be hard, but it's the hard things that tend to be the most rewarding and enduring in life.

At my lowest point, after my son died, I really dove into my faith journey and turned it on full steam ahead. There was that part of me that just wanted to shut off, get drunk, give up, or hide from the world, but I knew enough to distrust those sorts of voices. Getting up and doing the right thing was what was necessary, and by the grace of God, that's what I did.

Getting out of my life of crime was hard and incon-venient. I had a long period of not making much money. Getting out of prison, quitting the motorcycle club, dropping every contact and resource I had, and facing the world with two little kids was the hardest time in my life. But I am glad that I made those changes for my children's sake. I ended up reaping the benefits as well. When life was tragic and empty, I was tempted to stuff it all inside and let myself slowly decay, but by the grace of God, I listened to the good Lord's calling instead. I am glad that I got back in the faith. It is what made me well when I was really questioning the order and meaning of life. And the timing was impeccable because, the minute I got recalibrated and back in the groove, I heard those three little words you never want to hear: "You have cancer."

It's always something, folks. If you don't have money, you may have money related problems. If you do have money, life will find something else to throw at you. But if you have peace, if you have an understanding with your Maker, if you diligently work toward the right kind of goals, nothing can knock you down for too long. It's like Charles Swindoll said, "Life is 10 percent what happens to me and 90 percent how I react to it." The same is true for you and me.

The doctors who diagnosed my cancer told me it was routine, by the way. They said, "Hey, don't be alarmed. We see this stuff from time to time," and I thought, "Really?! Don't be alarmed, got it." But fortunately, I had the surgery, and it was successful. I still have to pay attention, obviously, but they were able to carve it all out, and the cancer had not metastasized or anything like that. So, I dodged another bullet. I'm not done yet.

Now, I'm going to talk just a little bit more about faith, and I know that not all of you reading this book are particularly inclined to hear about that sort of thing, but I urge you to give me a chance. Just because we avoid the great questions in life doesn't mean that we haven't picked a side. Just because we think we're too tough, it doesn't mean that we don't need strength and help. For me, God has become my strength. I used to think I wasn't afraid of anybody. Now, I have a relationship with God, and I just want to say that I'm better for it.

One of the things that got me through my battle with cancer and all that accompanying anxiety was prayer. I knew that when I called out, someone was listening, and whether God answered my prayers the way I wanted Him to or not, I could trust that He was going to do the right thing. When I pray, I talk to God as if I'm talking to a friend like Tom or Ron, asking for wisdom and guidance just like when I used to talk to them.

One of the things that has happed with Eric being gone is that I'm not concerned about dying anymore. I now know that when that happens, I get to be with my son again. I'm not really looking forward to death, but there's no downside anymore, you know? When my number gets called, I'll be ready. Until then, God and I have this little arrangement – If He wakes me up to see another day, I promise to try and be better than I was yesterday.

I've read some more books. I even read Blanchard's *Lead Like Jesus* a second time. I have this voracious appetite for learning about the faith and trying to live by scripture, and I can't get enough of it. Pastor Harold from the East County Transitional Living Center told me once that for a lot of people, their faith journey is like a life journey: First you're an infant, then you want more and more, and you become a teenager – and nobody can tell you anything, because you already know it all, right? And then you get to the point where you realize, "You know, gee, I really don't know anything." That is when you really mature in the faith.

I think I'm probably in that "can't get enough of it" phase.

## The Lesson from My Life

I get choked up thinking about this. It's hard to describe, and some of it will be reiterating themes I've written about earlier in this book, but I will do my best to put it all together for you.

Everything that I used to think mattered... is not what matters. I wanted to be the baddest of the bad because that's how I grew up, and that's the path I took. Obviously, that's not the best way. It nearly killed me, and it left me without anything to show for all that trouble. And then I thought it was important to be a corporate titan and to win constantly, that no matter what, I'm going to be driven and successful.

Well, I got everything I asked for, and it was like gravel in my mouth.

Skip ahead several years, and now I have peace. I attribute this entirely to learning about the Lord and what matters, and what our purpose here in life is. Our purpose isn't to get rich or to run businesses and corporations that impress everyone; our purpose is to help a brother out. Figuring out how our God-given talents can be used to help each other is what really matters. That's why I'm so happy today, because I do as much of that as I can.

I know that we have choices, and I know that the decisions that I made were my own. When I lived on the dark side, I was choosing that with full knowledge of what I was getting into and how likely it was that I would die in it. But I didn't die, and I believe that I survived it for a reason.

There were a couple of times where I should have died. I've had to be vague on the details, but take my word for it. And there were a couple of times that I should have gotten a life sentence in the penitentiary, but because of some technicalities, I was able to get past it. But let there be no doubt about it, the road I was on only had two destinations: One was the penitentiary, and the other was the cemetery.

Many people face these seemingly overwhelming challenges of wondering where their station in life is and trying to figure out the way forward when they feel like all is lost; they're branded with the scarlet letter, and, "Check the box. I'm a felon." I have an uncommon sympathy and experience to be able to reach brothers and sisters who are in that place. To be able to shine a little light at that time, that's why I survived this stuff. I'm alive and talking about it, helping others through it.

If you're reading this book, I can't help but notice that you're alive too. Do you know why the good Lord kept you from dying all these years? Because I promise there is a good reason.

It's a faithful saying that the two most important days in your life are the day you were born and the day you find out why. I know now that my purpose is to break the cycles of recidivism, addiction, and poverty for whoever is willing to listen. I want to let everyone crawling out of the dark know that it is not too late to start over.

The best time to plant an apple tree is five years ago. The second-best time is today.

That's my story and my purpose.

What's yours?

-    M.

*"What we do for ourselves dies with us. What we do for others and the world remains and is immortal."*
-   Anonymous

# Acknowledgements

By the odds and all statistics, I should not be writing this. The road I was on had but two destinations: the penitentiary and the cemetery. It is only by God's mercy and grace that I did not wind up in one of those places forever. As the good Lord looked over me, there have also been some good folks that have come alongside and helped me on my journey, to whom I owe enormous appreciation. The first I will mention is Wesley Fulkerson, who agreed to partner with me on writing this book. When it comes to this project, it is Wes who has done all of the heavy lifting as I sat predominately on the sidelines.

On the San Diego Waterfront, Tom Wright was my first boss, and he was my friend at a time when I needed a friend the most. Without Tom's friendship and counsel at a most pivotal time in my life, I would never have made it off of parole. Jim Clark was the first of several mentors that had enough faith and confidence in me to provide me with opportunities that I would have never thought I was ready for. Marty Fischer taught me the business of how to manage people, time, and money. Bob Koerber, a quiet giant who taught me how to lead and what it was to be a leader long before I knew anything about servant leadership.

There have also been a few truly exceptional souls who risked heaven and earth to be my partner in business. Mark Withers, with whom I have enjoyed the most complementary professional relationship (like Yin and Yang, we are the perfect balance); Richard Bartlett-May, my close friend and confidant; Cyndi Spell, with whom I grew up on the waterfront. We worked together, raised our kids together, and had a whole lot of fun together! Who knew when we started out that we would build a business that would be bought by the former Secretary of the Navy, J. F. Lehman, a private equity investor?

I can only count them on one hand, but these are the titans that have been there for me anytime of the day or night, who will drop everything without ever even asking why. Elliot Wittes, Jeff Boguskie, Dave Larson, and Duane Fitzpatrick: I will be forever grateful and in your debt. It has been my privilege to have you in my corner.

My brother Mike, whom I shared a bedroom with by the railroad tracks. You have been there for me since we were children and every day since. I cannot adequately express the depth of my most sincere gratitude for the unwavering love and support you have provided me my entire life.

My wife Lyndy: I never thank you enough for your encouragement and for being my greatest supporter.

- Marcel Becker, February 2021

# Did You Love This Book?

Here are some ways you can help spread the word:

- Leave a five-star review on Amazon, Goodreads, or wherever you find your books online.

- Book Marcel to come and speak to your local recovery program, church congregation, school, chamber of commerce, or other organization by sending an email to

  WAFulkersonBooks@gmail.com

  with the subject line: "Book Marcel Becker"

- Ask your favorite podcasts and radio shows to interview Marcel.

- Tell your friends, pass your copy along, or email

  WAFulkersonBooks@gmail.com

  to inquire about reduced prices for bulk orders.